Testimonials

What others are saying about this book:

"Great stories by a great lady! People like Venna Bishop have made the "glories" the tremendous productions they have become over the years.
Right on!"
Roger Williams – Mr. Piano

"True stories always get your attention. When it's true stories about a high profile event that's known world wide, that really gets and holds your attention."
**Danny Cox – Acceleration Unlimited
"The sonic boom salesman"**

"Having been to several "Glories," I've had the delight of listening to a little lamb "singing" along with the shepherd, of laughing at the beautiful tiger swatting the leg of Pilate, of watching in amazement as angels soared above the Cathedral, and of emotionally experiencing the birth, life, death, and resurrection of Jesus

Christ. But the "Glory Stories" bring me to a new level of appreciation as Venna takes us behind the scenes. Weaving moments of humor, tenderness, love and insights from her "angel's point of view," she has captured the heart and purpose of the "Glories . . . telling the story of Jesus."

Gail Wenos – Gail & Ezra Ministries
Gail Wenos, ventriloquist

"IF I WAS A ANGEL AND LANDED ON TOP OF DR. SCHULLER'S HEAD, I WOULDA SHOUTED, 'THIS ARE THE DAY THAT THE LORD HAS MADE, AND I IS GONNA REJOICE AND BE GLAD IN IT' JESUS WOULDA LOVED IT!"

EZRA D. PEABODY (SMART DUMMY)
Gail & Ezra Ministries

GLORY
STORIES

Second Edition

Uplifting Narratives Sparkling with Joy and Faith

It's Not How You Fly, It's How You LAND!

by Venna Bishop

Pos I Publishing ~San Jose, California

Glory Stories

It's Not How You Fly, It's How You LAND!

by Venna Bishop

Published by:
Pos I Publishing
Post Office Box 700443
San Jose, CA 95170-0443
orders: posipub@earthlink.net

Editor – Emily De Shazo
Graph Designer – Purple Cat Productions - Catharine Foresman
Photographer – Claudia Holloway
Glory Angel Logo – used by permission of Paul David Dunn, Producer/Director
Please see acknowledgements at the back of the book for complete attribution for material used in this book.

Unless indicated Scripture quotations are from *Possibilities Thinkers Bible*, the New King James Version © 1984 Executive Editor Robert H. Schuller Commentaries by Paul David Dunn – Thomas Nelson Publishers

LCCN 2006903240
Library of Congress Cataloging-in-Publication Data
Glory Stories: witty, uplifting narratives sparkling with hope and joy / Venna Bishop
p.cm
ISBN 0-9773893-1-6   ISBN 978-09773893-1-6
1. Christian life   I. Venna Bishop, date
© 2007 by Venna Bishop
Second Edition

Published in the United States of America

Foreword

by Dr. Robert H. Schuller

Venna Bishop's collection of "Glory Stories" is a tribute to the volunteers and staff who participated in and supported the Glory of Christmas and Glory of Easter for over the past twenty-five years. This book contains a wonderful collection of wisdom and insight. There are moments of humor accented by laughter that will bring smiles to anyone who has ever participated in or attended a performance. You will identify with the unpredictable behaviors, challenges, and antics of working with live animals. The endless possibilities of transforming the Crystal Cathedral into a theater venue and the teamwork and commitment involved, are truly special. Hearts will be touched by the inspiring thoughts of the flying angels as they soared above audiences' eyes and hearts. Every reader will find at least one story that is meaningful to them – one story to treasure and share.

This book

is dedicated

to **YOU** the **AUDIENCE**

and to everyone who has been led to Christ

by attending the

Glory of Christmas and Glory of Easter

pageants.

Contents

THE GLORY OF
REALIZING A
DREAM

It's Not How You Fly, It's How You LAND!

Have you ever had your purpose or direction in life shaken? I did! To boost my spirits my best friend, Marilyn Blum, suggested we drive to Southern California to see the Glory of Christmas pageant at the Crystal Cathedral. I was thrilled and ready for something uplifting. Driving onto the Cathedral grounds was like entering paradise. There were twinkling lights in the trees and red poinsettias throughout the campus. It was absolutely heavenly! Thoughts of the devastating collapse of my twenty-five year marriage fell by the wayside. There were so many friendly ushers welcoming us and shaking our hands. Once inside the Cathedral, I was dazzled by the expanse of the Bethlehem set and the beautifully draped garlands around the ledges of the balcony.

Sitting in the audience that night, I had no idea of the impact this pageant would have on the rest of my life. Jim Nabor's baritone rendition of "O Holy Night" reached into my soul. My heart was filled with joy as the pageant continued with the music of "Hark, the Herald Angels Sing." The 90-foot door of the Cathedral opened to the outdoors exposing real clouds and stars. Simultaneously, a Flying Angel appeared above the manger and flew against a background of real stars in the night sky. The Angel's face was radiant with light. She was smiling and looking right at me! My heart began to pound and my soul was lifted upward by the graceful movement of her wings. In that moment, I felt empowered by the Spirit of God with an angelic purpose. I was to become a Flying Angel. Nothing, absolutely nothing, would stop me from pursuing this God inspired idea and intention for my life.

After the finale, I settled back into the pew and said to my friend, "Marilyn, I am going to be one of those flying angels someday."

Marilyn quickly responded and said, "But, Venna, you have short brown hair."

I shrugged my shoulders, glanced her way, and continued, "God created angels with short and long hair, blond and brown hair, youthful angels and some are more mature, with brown hair, like me. I just know, someday I will find a way to be one of those Flying Angels."

When I returned to my home in San Jose, California, I cut a picture of one of the Flying Angels out of the "Possibilities Magazine" along with a quote from Dr. Robert H. Schuller, "Build a Dream and the Dream Will Build You." I taped the picture and quote to my refrigerator door. (The angel in the picture was Geri Enderle, the same person I saw flying in the pageant. Geri had cancer and passed away soon after the pageant.) I manifest things in my life through visualization and by maintaining a positive attitude. The special picture and quote continue to serve as symbols of my dreams and goals. They provide encouragement and focus for all my endeavors.

The next three years were wrought with challenges as I began to pursue my dream. My paid position as a Job Developer for Santa Clara County, in Northern California, was grant-funded and the funding was running out. So I began interviewing and was selected for a position with a new company. Six weeks later, I was fired! I was being rejected again, first in my marriage, and then in my new job. To my surprise, those rejections paved the way for new opportunities.

The next summer I contacted the Cathedral to learn what was required to be a flying angel. The switchboard operator connected me with a friendly administrator in public relations named Claudia Holloway, who had flown as an angel. Claudia was a true inspiration to me, an encourager. She informed me of the 118 pound weight restriction and the dance-clothing requirement for the auditions. She even connected me with Jan Wacker McCurry, who was contemplating opening a Hawaiian Bed & Breakfast in her home. (I would need a place to stay the night of auditions.) Claudia ended the conversation by saying, "I'll see you at the auditions."

The auditions were my first challenge, especially when I saw all the teenagers who were stretching out in the auditioning room. It helped to meet Claudia when I arrived. Nevertheless, it was still scary for me, a "mature adult" pushing 50, to wear leotards and tights and learn dance routines the minute we arrived for auditions. The teenage competitors were certainly more agile at dance routines and movements than I was. I was raised on an Arlington, Nebraska, farm and ballet lessons were not offered in school or as one of my 4-H projects. Certainly, swinging from ropes in my father's hay barn would give me an edge when it came to flying. Making the best of a challenging situation, I positioned myself behind the best dancer, memorized the dance sequence and smiled brilliantly no matter what my feet were doing. When I heard I was selected to be one of the angels who would fly 90 feet in the air at 40 miles an hour, I think I could have flown without wires or wings!

After auditioning, the second greatest challenge was the commute between my home in

San Jose, and the Crystal Cathedral in Garden Grove, California. For six months, I traveled 800 miles, round trip, two or three times a week for rehearsals and performances. At the time I had a full time job as Personnel Recruitment Specialist for two colleges focusing on nationwide recruitment for faculty and staff.

On rehearsal days I would go to work at 6:00 AM and leave at 3:00 PM, then drive directly to the San Jose airport. After parking my car, I would fly to Los Angeles International Airport and catch a shuttle to the Disneyland Hotel. (Jan Wacker McCurry, the owner of the bed and breakfast, became my dear close friend, whom I later dubbed a Saint.) Jan would meet me at the hotel and drive me to the Cathedral for two hours of rehearsal. After rehearsal she would arrive to take me to meet the shuttle. It was the reverse procedure going home. If everything went smoothly, it was only a seven-hour commute.

Each time I set foot on the Cathedral grounds, I would become fully energized. I overflowed with joy and was thrilled to be part of a cast of 200 dedicated volunteers. We were each a vital part of the team's endeavor. This included everyone from Roman soldiers to shepherds, technicians to ushers. This energy lifted me out of my daily drab routine, recharged my spiritual batteries and distributed sparks of joy to the people I met in route.

Finally, it was opening night. The child in me was filled with anticipation. I was standing high above the west balcony, balancing myself on a platform no bigger than a saucer, awaiting my cue. The trumpets sounded and music filled the Cathedral. I felt the harness tighten and pinch against my body. Suddenly, my wings took flight and gave me lift. There was light all around me. As the wind raced past my cheeks, I looked down into the eyes of children. They were smiling and waving at me. People were sitting in church pews and wheel chairs, their mouths open in astonishment, just as mine had been three years before. It had come to pass; I was SOARING ON THE WINGS OF MY DREAM! My God inspired dream had become a reality. I WAS AN ANGEL!

Great dreams are never just fulfilled; usually they exceed our expectations! The special story of my commitment and dedication, as the only angel volunteer who did not live in Southern California, prompted an invitation from Marjorie Kelley, Dr. Robert H. Schuller's secretary, to be an interview guest on his "Hour of Power" global television program. I was speechless! What would I have to say? What agenda had God planned for me to fulfill His purpose? When I looked at the lighted cross on the Tower of Hope at the Crystal Cathedral, I remembered a verse from Matthew 10:19-20 "Do not worry what you will say or how you will say it; the words you speak will not be yours; they will come from the Spirit of your Father speaking through you." The very next day, a production staff member had a clever idea to make this interview different from others. "Why don't we fly Venna in costume as an angel over the congregation and have her land for the interview?"

The day for the interview arrived, God had another surprise planned for us. With a twinkle in his eye, Dr. Robert H. Schuller stepped out to one side of the lectern and announced, "This morning, I think I will interview an Angel! I can't wait to say, 'God loves you and so do I' to an Angel." Simultaneously, my crew of angel pilots launched me out of the west balcony of the Cathedral. As I flew over the congregation toward the lectern, I could see that Dr. Schuller was completely absorbed and was paying little or no attention to my descent. In fact, he was innocently standing right on my angelic landing spot. I had no choice and no control over my landing. The wires and controls were in the hands of my angel pilots who follow a set script. To everyone's amazement, Dr. Schuller suddenly disappeared underneath my skirts as I landed RIGHT ON

TOP OF HIM! When he came out from under the yards and yards of fabric in my angelic gown, the TV cameras were rolling. He smoothed his silver hair, quickly turned, covered his red face in embarrassment, and gave me a big hug. He rose above his embarrassment with his cheerful spontaneous comment, "Now I know what angels wear!" (See cover photos)

My enthusiasm soared to new heights when I was flying as an angel. To continue meant auditioning twice a year for the Glory of Easter and Christmas pageants. Previous involvement did not guarantee being chosen again. I wanted to do everything I could to assure my selection. I was fully committed. It would take some extra effort on my part, so I enrolled in some ballet classes. It was inspiring to proclaim good news as an angelic messenger, while moving my arms in slow graceful ports-de-bras.

After two years of coping with a hectic commute schedule, I resigned my recruitment position and created a sales career out of being a volunteer. I became a wholesale manufacturer's representative focusing on angel product lines. Before long, clients called me the "Angel Lady Rep!" I made sales calls, while traveling between my home and the Cathedral for rehearsals and performances. It was during the International Women's Conference at the Cathedral, I met

Katherine (Kitty) Paladin, who agreed to rent me a room in her home for some of my commutes. She became a great friend and enjoyed teasing me for being a "fly by night."

A routine mammogram in 1989 detected a lump, and a team of surgeons recommended operating. The night before surgery I teasingly said, "It is just my angel wings growing a little farther forward than before!" I assured them these wings came out every fall and folded up in the spring after the Easter pageants. One of the surgeons chuckled, having graduated from the University of California at Irvine, he was familiar with the Flying Angels in Crystal Cathedral's pageants. The next morning the surgeon's did another ultrasound and learned the lump was moving. This meant I had other options, since cancerous lumps do not move. I told them, "You don't need practice in surgery and I don't need practice in healing." Besides, I have Flying Angel rehearsals to attend.

After checking myself out of the hospital, I decided to make a sales call before going home. I started driving my car toward the Cypress area of Oakland, California. Suddenly, it seemed rather warm in the car. It felt like something heavy landed on my shoulders. I was concerned and stopped the car along the side of the road. Looking around and seeing nothing, I realized I was emotionally exhausted. Perhaps this was the Lord's way of getting my attention and protecting me. It was only a few hours later when the Oakland Bay Bridge and the Cypress ramp exit collapsed during the 7.0 earthquake.

My involvement as a Flying Angel was two-fold. I was invited to be a luncheon speaker, along with Buddy Adler* (King Herod), by Sharon Hunter the manager for Travel Possibilities. Sharon Hunter organized tour groups from around the world to visit the Cathedral and attend the pageants. Before they departed for home on Sundays, she had a luncheon where Buddy and I told the story of our involvement in the pageants. Sometimes we shared the platform with Dr. Robert H. Schuller or Paul David Dunn, the Producer/Director. It was this speaking opportunity, which helped launch my speaking career on the topic, "It's Not How You Fly, It's How You LAND!"

My passion for being a Flying Angel volunteer prevailed for five years, before I made the decision to stop. It was NOT an easy choice for it had been my dream. I struggled and shed some tears, after deciding I was not going to audition anymore. My wings and halo were lifting me another direction. It was time to focus and pursue my life long dream of being a professional speaker. I needed to let go and leave my "heavenly nest." I HAD EARNED MY WINGS! They would always be a part of me whether I was soaring on land or in the air.

THE GLORY OF PRODUCTION

In the Beginning

How did the first Glory of Christmas evolve? It began by networking and connecting people with similar interests. Bob Jani was Entertainment Director at Disneyland, and was a producer/director at Radio City Music Hall, and for various football halftime shows. He was also an avid collector of Christian art and wanted to produce a Christmas show using his art.

Sheldon Disrud, the former choral director at the Cathedral, knew of Bob Jani's idea and he also knew Bob Schuller was interested in producing a Christmas pageant in the Crystal Cathedral. Sheldon arranged for the "two Bob's," along with Arvella Schuller, to have lunch at Club 33 to discuss possibilities.

Agreement was reached when a third Bob, namely Bob Krogstead, Director of Music at the Cathedral joined the 'Bob' team. The first musical tracks for the Glory of Christmas were arranged and orchestrated by Bob Krogstead with members of the London Symphony Orchestra. After Bob Krogstead returned from London with the music, Sheldon selected twenty-four members from his choir. During the next week, they spent every evening singing those choral numbers. Their choral music was recorded over several times and added to the musical track for the first production of the Glory of Christmas.

Soloists were also included. Debby Smith Tebay sang "Sleep, Holy Child," with Fred Frank singing "O Holy Night." The song "The Little Drummer Boy" was sung by Mark Simmons.

Bob Jani produced and directed the pageant by incorporating some of his religious art to portray the various Christmas scenes along with the music. Charles Fowler was the narrator.

The 'Bob' team made it happen in 1981, improvements were made, and twenty-five years later more than 3 million people from around the world have attended the pageants.

In this behind-the-scenes account of the pageants, you will read about animal antics, horse tales, and a peacock's lifeless performance. You will be touched by the on-stage epiphany of a child's healing, a disciple's audition, and the commitment of entire families. You will chuckle at an innkeeper's compensation, a child wrangler's shortcomings, an angels 'surprise landing' that launched a speaking and writing career—It's Not How You Fly, It's How You LAND!"

From Holy Land to Glory Land

Paul David Dunn lived in the Muslim Quarter of Jerusalem near the Damascas Gate for five years. He studied in the Holy Land as a New Testament scholar, having received an International Rotary Graduate Scholarship for postgraduate studies in archeology, historical geography, and international relations. Paul is fluent in the Arabic language and he organized and directed programs for students throughout the Sinai wilderness. Paul also worked on archeological digs with scientists and gained his scholarly reputation through his academic articles and lectures at Stanford University and the Rockefeller Museum.

Paul lived and hiked where Jesus walked. He has an appreciation for the terrain and climatic conditions people living in Biblical times must have experienced. He worked on a major six-hour documentary, filmed on location in Israel, as TV production consultant on the Middle East. In 1982 Dr. Robert H. Schuller hired Paul whose first-hand experiences made him the ideal person to tell the Christmas and Easter stories in a script that was true to Biblical accounts.

Paul admits 'he had a little help from the disciples,' since the scripts Paul wrote for both pageants are taken from the Bible. The basic story line remains consistent for each pageant with changes occurring in details each year. Whether it involves new music, set changes or choreographic embellishments, the goal is to bring every facet of the show out into the audience—to make the audience feel they are a part of what is happening on stage.

Imagine hiking in the Holy Land and experiencing first-hand the living conditions and seasonal climate changes. It was obvious to Paul David Dunn that the journey Mary and Joseph made from Nazareth to Bethlehem would have taken at least seven days. Weather at that time of the year could have reached 90 to 100 degrees. Electrical storms were prevalent, so thunder and lightning were introduced to create an in-house electrical storm during Mary and Joseph's journey to Bethlehem.

Bringing a touch of realism to the pageants are the live animals. One year Paul added two tethered wolves at the top of the shepherds' hill. It seemed natural that shepherds tending the campfires and protecting their sheep would be faced with predators intimidating their flocks. According to cast members the male and female wolves were huge, nearly the size of a large German Shepherd dogs. Unfortunately, it was also the wolves' mating season, and they were quickly excused from performing in the remaining shows. Paul enjoys adding more exotic animals to the productions. There have been lions lounging at King Herod's feet and tigers and jaguars in Pontius Pilate's court.

The set, designed by Charles Lisanby, consists of 5 miles of steel under-girding that is necessary to hold a cast of 200 volunteers and professional actors, dancers, and animals. In 1986, Paul set King Herod's Court on a platform next to the East balcony landing. The following year he had a special platform built 50 feet above the main floor for the prophets from the Old Testament. (Paul is rather mysterious about the prophets' ascent to their platform.) The Glory of Christmas stage has over 3000 lights in the backdrop, depicting stars that are attached by hand during preparation for the pageant. The set spans 124 feet across the front of the Cathedral. It is 80 feet high, and is one of the largest indoor stage sets in the world. Paul's desire was to create a set so realistic that audience members would feel as if they were stepping back in time to a place where they were participating in these Biblical events.

Paul conducted extensive research of the period in order to design authentic costumes and props. Even the sandals on the cast members' feet are in accordance with those worn by Jesus and His disciples. The dance choreography combines modern ballet with Jewish folk dancing. Every effort is made to keep all aspects of the show historically accurate. The imagination is shown with the angels, since Paul can't recruit actual angels. Yet, all of us who have flown as angels, believe Paul has given us an opportunity to be the angelic messengers God wants us to be by proclaiming His good news to all who come.

In Jerusalem, Paul David Dunn met Jeanne Schuller (Robert and Arvella Schuller's second daughter). Paul and Jeanne went from dating in the Holy Land to getting married in Garden Grove, California. Since then they have worked together continuously on the Glory productions. Jeanne served as editor for the "Possibilities" magazine and continues to work with the Glory staff on publicity for the pageants while raising a family. She has been the Assistant Producer for the pageants and is currently the Associate Director. The pageants have added over one million dollars to the ministry's mission funds.

While Paul admits the story line doesn't

change, the pageants have new details added every year. Together, he and Jeanne strive to blend historical authenticity with theatrical magic.

As Producer/Director for the Glory of Christmas and the Glory of Easter, Paul David Dunn is especially grateful for the thousands of dedicated and volunteers who have been a part of these productions for the past twenty-five years. The tireless support of the staff and volunteers who have given hours of their time has contributed to the success of the pageants, and to the overall mission of the Crystal Cathedral to reach those people who do not know Jesus yet.

The Inner Workings of the Glory Staff

How does a Glory Staff member stay physically fit? Undoubtedly, it begins by walking down the 39 steps to go to work in their offices, located under the sanctuary of the Crystal Cathedral. The Glory Office is the very first door on the left at the west end of the lower concourse. During rehearsals and shows the staff members easily stay in shape zipping up and down stairs attending to details in a Cathedral that spans the length of two football fields. The days from September to June are busy and bustling with activity. Their hours are significantly longer during the sixteen weeks of rehearsals and shows. Summer is more relaxed and a welcome reprieve.

Sandy Boselo has been a part of the staff since 1987. "It's like having an extended family," Sandy says. "When the rest of the staff and the volunteers return in the fall, it's great to reconnect with everyone again. There is a feeling of belonging, a caring and sharing that comes with being a part of something that has value."

Sandy went on to say, "Each year we have

some new volunteers so the family keeps growing and changing. Some previous cast members pursue new endeavors, move away or have passed on to a better place. There remains those dedicated individuals, with wonderful hearts, who keep returning and inspire all of us."

Before joining the Glory staff, Sandy worked in finance in the retail industry. It was the message the Glory productions convey that called her to seek a position in the Glory office. Through the years she has held almost every position from being a part time receptionist to her current position as production coordinator. Sandy is in charge of finance and accounting relating to advertising, purchasing, and payroll. Each show requires new contracts for the staff and all of the performers. Audition schedules for the various speaking parts, dancers, and angel casting are coordinated. Resumes are reviewed and invitations to audition are extended. The auditions and call-backs require the support and participation of various members of the Glory staff. Previous participants in the general cast are sent letters announcing sign-ups, followed by announcements in the church bulletin.

Working with Sandy for twelve years was another staff member Cindi Palomarez. Cindi was part of the Glory staff handling public relations until she left to spend more time with her family.

I recall when Margit Larson was on staff. She asked Sandy Asche, and I to accompany her to Leisure World at Laguna Niguel to be interviewed on their local television station to promote the pageants.

Kathy Black was on staff the first year I performed. She wrote an article about my roundtrip commute of 800 miles for rehearsals and performances to be a flying angel volunteer for the "Possibilities" magazine. The editor for this magazine of hope was Jeanne Dunn.

Presently joining Sandy Boselo in many of these endeavors is Cathy Dixon. Cathy focuses on public relations. She works with Jeanne Dunn on the publicity and is the assistant to producer/director, Paul David Dunn.

Prior to joining the Glory office, Cathy worked in the same building the Hour of Power offices were located. Her familiarity with the Hour of Power proved an asset. Cathy coordinates with wardrobe and arranges for cast members to participate in Sunday services to promote the pageants aired on the Hour of Power. She sends out promotional materials, press releases, and invites the media to attend the pageants. Sometimes a radio or television personality will agree to do a small segment of a rehearsal and report their experiences to their listening audience.

Tony Ewing, with the radio broadcast "Good

Day LA," agreed to ride a camel as King Caspar during a Glory of Christmas rehearsal. What Tony didn't realize was the camel would "cush" (sit down), when the procession reached the manger. Tony's camel started to "cush" by kneeling down on its front legs, which threw Tony off balance. His headdress and wig fell off, while his voice rose at least two octaves. It took a minute before the camel could kneel down on its hind legs and tuck them underneath its body into a level sitting position. Tony soon realized his camel riding experience would also generate chuckles with his co-workers at the radio station.

Sandy Boselo and Cathy Dixon coordinate with all of the departments and provide support as needed for the producer/director. Cathy also prepares media kits, organizes photo shoots, gathers and assembles information that goes into the pageant programs. Sandy recalled a rehearsal when Alan Coates*, who plays Pontius Pilate, started speaking his lines using his John Wayne accent. Alan's out-of-character accent added a humorous twist to an evening's rehearsal. Sandy and Cathy also rotate with other staff members as primary contacts in the Glory office during the sixteen-week run of the shows.

Imagine busloads of 13,000 school children, arriving on Children's Day to see the Glory of Christmas each year. Children's Day is the only daytime show. It is a favorite with cast members, who are able to take time off from their jobs. Requests from schools and charities outnumber the available seating, so selection is determined by a lottery system. Cathy assumes the task of notifying the "winners" and extending those invitations.

For the past twenty-five years, over 3 million people have attended the pageants. The staff, cast members, and all the volunteers involved in the production have received accolades from around the world. Videos, tapes, CD's, and DVD's of the pageants have been produced to share the music and drama of the miracles . . . the parables . . . the life . . . of an innocent Christ Child born to bring God's salvation to the world.

Tribute to Terry Larson

Terry Larson was an integral part of the Glory production staff from its inception. As assistant director, Terry was the pivotal element that kept every facet of the pageants operating smoothly. Given any task, Terry made it happen 'with style' beyond anyone's expectations. A stage manager once referred to Terry as "the show in a box." He was highly respected by cast members and staff, and had their profound gratitude for his personal attention to their needs. Terry was present and available at every single audition, rehearsal, and performance. He had a way of overcoming challenges and an instant witty comment to lighten the moment. His sudden passing in the spring of 2002 left a void within the staff and in the volunteers' hearts. His ingenious mind, creative talents, and humorous responses are missed. Perhaps he is now assisting and directing another glorious production in paradise.

THE GLORY OF PUBLIC RELATIONS

The Launching Pad

The Glory of Christmas began with an idea. A team was formed to create the script, music and set. A request was placed in the church bulletin for volunteers to be in the cast and auditions were scheduled. Before there could be an audience, a "launching pad" or reservations center was needed to make it happen. A ticket is necessary for one to attend a pageant and the reservations center was the primary launch site for ticket sales for the past twenty-five years. The current Reservations Manager, Sharon Hunter, has been a part of that launch pad team since its inception. During those 25 years, over three million tickets were issued to attend the pageants.

Cathy Leestma was the first Reservations Manager. Her launch team consisted of her assistant Lois Pearson, group sales coordinator Sharon Hunter, and Emilie Schultz Webb who worked part time taking ticket orders. It is amusing now to recall a comment made by a key staff member who was picking up tickets and said, "I can't imagine this pageant lasting more then one season, since everyone already knows the story. Why would anyone want to come again?"

For many, attending the pageants is a family tradition. There are families who begin their Christmas season by attending the pageant. Sharon said, "We have one family that reserves a dozen seats in the first row every year. They started bringing their children and now they bring their grandchildren."

Employees at the Cathedral also like to be involved in the pageant in some other capacity. Lois Pearson eventually became manager of the Reservations Center and was also a flying angel one season. Some nights she did a little 'ground flying,' racing between her launch pad at the reservation center to the angel loft. Sharon Hunter managed Travel Possibilities for four years arranging weekend tour packages for people from around the world to attend the pageants, before taking charge as Reservations Manager of the reservations center.

With construction going on around the Cathedral campus through the years, the reservations center has been moved innumerable times. Sometimes the move occurred at the beginning of the launch season for ticket sales or even in the middle of an event. Through the years managers have dealt with various computerized ticketing systems. Mangers also spend time interviewing and training 15 to 25 part time people to handle ticket sales each season. Some people return each season to work part time. Much to Sharon's delight, approximately one third of her part time people have gone on to find full time positions within the ministry. Sharon is excited about the dimension of Internet "live ticketing" that will be available in 2006. Reservations can be made on line and patrons will be able to print their own tickets at their own computers.

Twenty-five years ago, Sharon had just become a Christian. She read in the bulletin they were hiring for a new production called the Glory of Christmas. Sharon admitted, "I was divorced and really needed a job to support myself and my two children." After being hired she recalled a verse from Hebrews 13:5 "I will never leave you nor forsake you." Sharon said, "Each year has provided me an opportunity to build a closer and closer relationship with the Lord. He totally took over my life." Sharon continued, "I don't look at being the Reservations Manager as a job. I thoroughly enjoy what I do. I really look forward to going to work every day. I look forward to making a difference in somebody else's life."

It is meaningful when someone calls for a

reservation for one of the pageants and shares how they were flipping through the TV channels and were touched by this ministry. Here are some of those comments:

"It's been my dream to fly out and see the Glory of Christmas," or

"I have cancer but I want to see the Crystal Cathedral before I die." or

"The minister spoke to me when I was ready to commit suicide."

Another gratifying event occurred when Sharon was leading the weekend tours with Travel Possibilities. Lee Sevig from Ohio and Priscilla Sullivan from Boston met on one of the Glory of Easter weekend tours in 1986. A few years later they ended up at the Cathedral again, Priscilla from Boston was walking into the Cathedral for Sunday services and Lee, who had moved to Camarillo, was walking out of the Cathedral. Lunch and a romance blossomed. They have been married eight years and make several trips each year to see the pageants at the Cathedral. Their latest trip included a visit with Sharon after going to see the production of "Creation."

Sharon admits, "Working in reservations has its crazy times. We are a business and we deal with business situations. Sometimes people are not always understanding of what we can or cannot do." The team Sharon manages tries to give more than what is asked of them such as hotel and shuttle information along with pageant tickets. The staff wants to provide the same kind of information anyone might need when visiting an area.

Sharon wonders where her life would have been had she not applied for the job in reservations at the Cathedral. Sharon stated, "It might have taken me in different direction. I could have been a totally different person. This ministry has helped me and I want to give back to it because of what it has given me. I don't look at my paycheck. I don't look at my work as a job. I look at it as being a blessing!"

The Tower Lady

The tallest building on the Crystal Cathedral grounds is the Tower of Hope with its illuminated Cross stretching 19 stories above the ground. The glowing splendor of the Cross can be seen from miles away and is often used as a navigational landmark for pilots flying to and from Orange County's John Wayne Airport.

I imagine every Glory Angel flying, from the perch in the west balcony of the Cathedral, experienced some of the same emotions I did, when I launched forth from angel track number four. As we looked through the glass ceiling of the Crystal Cathedral, we were nearly as high as the base of the Cross on the Tower of Hope. The majestic glow emerging from the Cross was a beautiful reminder of God's purpose for us as human angels, and how fortunate and thankful we were to be sharing the good news of His birth and resurrection in this manner.

Located inside the Tower of Hope building was the Chapel in the Sky, a 24-hour counseling center, meeting rooms, pastoral and administrative offices. The Information Center and recep-

tion area filled the main floor and originally
served as the hub of the campus. A short and
perky lady, who spent 18 years behind a bustling Information Desk, with its busy phone lines
and sometimes congested reception area, (especially during performances) was BJ Scheid.
Some of us know her as BJ, while others referred to her as "The Tower Lady!"

BJ was drawn to angels and had accumu-
lated a unique collection of angel figurines,
statues, pictures, cards, and tiny treasures etc.
Her home was filled with shelves and cabinets
containing her favorites. Ushering at the Glory
Pageants and watching the angels fly was her
joy. How she would have loved to have flown
with us. Yet, she knew she would never make
the auditions. Spirit wise she would have been
at the top of the list but health wise and weight
wise, well, let's say, there were limitations. Then,
one evening as several of us were dashing up the
basement stairs with our angel costumes to pre-
set them in the west balcony before the building
opened, we met BJ at the back of the Crystal
Cathedral wearing her black usher's garb, waiting for the doors to open. Instantly I draped my
flying angel costume against her body. Angel
Debbie Zubiate assisted by slipping the fabric
wristbands, which were attached to the hem of
the skirt over BJ's wrist to create the effect of
wings. As I slipped behind BJ and ducked to

hold the dress part of the angel costume in place against her body, we had BJ lift her arms so the fabric, with its accordion pleats, fell into place and created the illusion of wings. In that moment, BJ, "The Tower Lady," became a land based Flying Angel!

Her land based Flying Angel incident was captured on camera and BJ was glowing as she shared her photo in an angel costume with Dr. Robert H. Schuller and his staff when she returned to work the next day as "The Tower Lady."

Penguins

The black and white attire required for an usher in the Glory of Christmas and Glory of Easter productions makes one think of a penguin. The Head Penguin is James B. Downs, more commonly known as Jim, the Head Usher. Approximately 40-50 penguin/ushers are needed each evening to greet, take tickets, and escort guests to their proper seats. It is amazing to see them in action between shows. They move much more quickly than real penguins. It only takes 18 minutes for the penguin/ushers to clear and seat 2200 guests between performances, in order that each show will start on time.

Before opening the doors of the Crystal Cathedral to the general public, the pengiun/ushers gather for devotions on the center ramp. Prayers are led by a Cathedral pastor, a staff member, or a volunteer. After devotions are finished, Jim provides the ushers with statistics regarding how many tickets were sold, the number of tour buses arriving, and any other special instructions. He playfully ends their time together with a joke of the day.

One evening, while the penguin/ushers were gathering on the center ramp for devotions, Jim was bubbling with excitement and told them to expect a 'surprise visitor.' Within seconds of his announcement, Jim received a radio signal that the 'surprise visitor' was in the area. An usher, Herbert Baker, rented a penguin costume, began waddling slowly down the center ramp.

Jim exclaimed, "As you can plainly see, our namesake has arrived!" The rest of the ushers were snickering and chuckling at the sight of the giant penguin coming toward them. Suddenly (without warning), Dr. Robert H. Schuller and Security's Bruce Hollenbeck, stepped out from behind the back curtain, much to Jim's astonishment. At the sight of Dr. Schuller, the penguin started sinking to his knees and nearly fainted. Jim was horror stricken, while Jim's supervisor, Joe Pardini, was extremely amused.

Dr. Schuller's wit captured the moment as his deep voice accentuated his comment, "My goodness, look what we have here. Did you come to pray with us, too?" Then Dr. Schuller had the ushers and penguin join hands, while he extended his personal thanks to them for their commitment to the ministry. When devotions ended, the penguin made an abrupt and speedy exit.

After the penguin episode, it did not surprise anyone when Jim was sporting a green cellophane derby on St. Patrick's Day, while sharing a little Irish wit. The ushers had finished seating the audience attending the Glory of Easter that evening and the opening scene began. The next scene was the beginning of Passover week, where Jesus enters the City of Jerusalem to cries of "Hosanna, Hosanna!" The disciples gathered in the lobby behind the curtain at the back of the center ramp waiting for their cue. Also entering the lobby, was Jesus riding the donkey named Hercules, more affectionately known by the cast as "Herkie."

Jim smirked as he plopped his green cellophane derby between Herkie's ears. "Be jibbers, ye gitten' in fashion," teased Jim. The cast and ushers standing in the lobby were chuckling at the sight. Suddenly, the cue came. Herkie obeyed and stepped forward from behind the curtain and up the ramp. It was like magic. The green derby quickly disappeared from Herkie's head and passed from the hand of Jesus back through the hands of each disciple before Jim realized what could have happened.

There are times when being an usher

around animals has its less glamorous moments. During the Glory of Christmas, there is the scene where Joseph and Mary are traveling from Nazareth to Bethlehem to be taxed. They stop and receive some water from a traveler. They continue by making a u-turn on the center ramp as a part of the journey. Mary was riding a donkey that would stop and urinate each time they made the u-turn. With three shows or four shows a night, the carpet became saturated. One of the ushers was standing near the u-turn spot. A few scenes later, flying angels appear announcing the birth of the Christ Child and dancers join in the celebration. The dancers run down the center aisle ramp executing beautiful ballet jumps. One of the dancers jumps and lands on the exact spot of the donkey's puddle pond—splattering liquid all over the poor usher. Imagine her surprise!

Guests and dancers sometimes have close encounters, too. One evening, a guest suddenly tried to leave during the performance. She barely reached the lobby, when everything from her stomach landed on the floor. Her timing paralleled that of the dancer's running exit down the center aisle ramp. The dancer's momentum coming off the ramp had her feet landing in the vomit of the bewildered guest. The dancer was even more dumbfounded, when she realized she was sitting in the middle of the guests' vomit. Fortunately, for the dancer and the usher assigned to the lobby, a "pooper scooper" cast member was instantly on the scene to clean up.

With a venue as large as the Cathedral, assigning people to cover all the entrances and balconies is important. One evening, when Stephanie Asche arrived, Jim Downs, head usher, assigned her to be one of four ushers in the East balcony. Stephanie was a lively young teenager and could easily hike up and down the balcony stairs to escort guests. Suddenly, things got very busy with busloads of people arriving. Jim completely forgot that Stephanie was the 'lone usher' in the East balcony, until after the pageant began. Later, he apologized and asked Stephanie how she managed to help everyone by herself.

Stephanie replied, "Oh, I cheated a little, because I couldn't seat each of guests personally. I just looked at their ticket and picked out someone wearing a bright colored blouse or a fancy tie and told them their seat was two rows up or three seats over from that individual. It was easy, once I found a few key people to focus on."

Jim admits in recent years Stephanie's approach has become valuable to him, since some maturity has rearranged his girth and stride.

After all, he says, "Stephanie's system beats ibuprofen and Ben Gay!"

Louis Massgengale, usher/coordinator, has been ushering for over twenty-five years at the pageants and church services. He enjoys meeting people from around the world. Like many of the ushers, he has exchanged cards, letters, and e-mail messages with many of the visitors he has met. Louis has some great answers for visitors most frequently asked questions.

When asked if the church has a bathroom, Louis replies, "Would you want to go to the bathroom in a glass church?" Then he directs them to the beautiful rest room area across the terrazzo. His cheery manner makes them smile and walking a few more steps to the rest room seems insignificant.

Another question that raises an eyebrow is when someone asks, "Where is the bar?"

A simple "Sorry, we don't have one." is the best response Louis can think of. "It helps to make them stop and consider where they really are."

Dick and Ruth Higgins sold programs the first few years they volunteered. Dick recalls when a young goat climbed up on a camel's hump during the show.

Dick said, "That goat must have thought he was in heaven standing on top of a camel's hump."

The Higgins took pleasure in meeting the visitors and hearing the "thank you" comments and blessings people felt after seeing the shows. Ruth has passed away, but Dick still finds joy in ushering and leading tours. Being a tour guide is a great way of sharing his Glory experiences firsthand.

For Frank Tillou, watching the pageants still has sentimental meaning even after years of ushering. Two songs in the Glory of Christmas continue to stir emotions for him. They are when Bradley Baker sings "O Holy Night" and when Debby Smith Tebay sings, " Sleep, Holy Child." However, last season he admitted Bridgette Bentley's rendition of "Mary, Did You Know?" was heart-wrenching. Frank enjoys the music in the pageants and at the Crystal Cathedral Sunday Services, where he also ushers. In the Glory of Easter, the songs "I Can See" and "Because He Lives" are especially meaningful to Frank.

First impressions are important to Ben and Jack Hadley. As greeters/coordinators they have been instrumental in providing a positive image for guests on the plaza courtyard before they enter the Cathedral. It is like welcoming guests in their home. Ben and Jack offer the first smile and first hand shake, that first feeling of warmth and acceptance that puts people at ease.

A great deal of pleasure and personal fulfill-ment comes from being an usher. Cast members frequently participate in the cast one evening and usher another evening. Sandie Morgan was a flying angel one night and would usher on another night. This provides a dual opportunity to witness to others and to experience these pageants from both perspectives.

Jim Downs sums it up best, "Being involved as an usher, guiding people along the way is the most rewarding thing I can do. There is no greater opportunity to further His works than to escort visitors through real-life enactments of the greatest story ever told. Some arrive hesitantly, thinking they are going to see a simple church play. They leave amazed and changed by the magnitude of the production."

Jim calls it, "Prevenient grace—God working in our lives and we don't even know it, until He brings us to where we can accept Christ. It involves everything that affects our lives, the good and the bad, the trials and the milestones. Everything comes together and when a person is ready, Christ is there! The Glory productions are a way of bringing forth Christ's anticipatory grace." Jim says, "That is why I usher, to serve Christ."

A Purple Heart

Joe Pardini was awarded a Purple Heart for his service and commitment at Iwo Jima during World War II. While recovering from his injuries, Joe met a young lady by the name of Äida operating the switchboard of Deca Records. It took several days before Joe got up enough nerve to ask her for a date, although his intuition told him that someday he would marry her. Tongue-tied in the beginning, but certainly at ease a few months later, Joe gave her a little purple box. Inside was his Purple Heart, symbolic of an engagement ring. Humbled by the gesture of receiving a Marine combat soldier's Purple Heart, Äida accepted his proposal and for the next 56° years Äida treasured Joe's Purple Heart (before leaving her earthly life to join the Heavenly Choir.)

Äida had a profound effect on Joe and a keen desire to sing in a choir. In 1976, when they moved to Buena Park, she suggested they attend the drive-in church in Garden Grove, but Joe refused. Joe was adamant, he didn't want anything to do with any church.

Then one day his boss, at the insurance company where he worked, invited him to a men's luncheon to hear Clement Stone speak. Little did Joe realize that the luncheon was on the drive-in church's campus. Imagine Joe's dilemma and frustration, which was only compounded when he accidentally stepped into one of the reflecting ponds on the church grounds. Immediately three ladies rushed over with red towels to dry him off. There he was with a wet trouser leg, his boss insisting it was not a church service, when who should get up to introduce the speaker, but the minister, Robert H. Schuller. Joe had no choice but to be quiet as he sat down in the very back row.

It wasn't long before he was totally engrossed in Clement Stone's speech. Now he was faced with his second plight of the day, what would he tell his wife? Without any hesitation when he arrived home he popped her a kiss and blurted out, "Guess where I was today?"

Äida just smiled and the following Sunday she turned on the television to the "Hour of Power" church service. As the choir sang Äida sighed and in a tantalizing way commented to Joe, "Do you hear that choir?"

Joe could see his wife was captivated and he replied, "You go ahead and sign up for the choir, and 'if you make it', I'll go to church."

Not only did Äida sign up and sing with

David Leestma's early morning 8:30 AM choir, but she also took singing lessons from David. Imagine her joy when she auditioned in the fall and was selected to be in the "big choir," as she referred to it.

With his wife singing in three services, what was Joe to do? Thus began Joe's involvement in the congregation as he started ushering for two of the church services and attended the Home Builders Sunday School Class. He became even more committed when he automatically agreed to usher for the Glory of Christmas followed by the Glory of Easter. Before he could even retire from his insurance career, he was approached to be the Head Usher and when Bill Carr retired Joe became the Cathedral's House Manager.

For nearly 30 years Joe Pardini has been ushering or managing the security for all of the daytime and evening events held inside the Crystal Cathedral. In addition to church services, this includes all special events such as, weddings, memorials, concerts, graduations, as well as the Glory of Christmas and Easter pageants and the newest pageant, Creation.

Joe's commitment and dedication parallels the service he gave as a Marine to his country. While his battle scars as a house manager are few, the joy and pride he had in watching his wife sing in the choir glistened through her lovely grey hair. On nights when Joe was overseeing the ushers at the Glory performances, Äida would be in the downstairs choir office sorting and filing music for the next choir rehearsal or Sunday service. Two dedicated individuals deserving of accolades and drawn to one another by a little box containing a Purple Heart, symbolic of their love for one another and for the Lord.

THE GLORY OF MUSIC

Keys, Pedals, & Stops

The Glory of Christmas officially begins with the playing of the prelude "In Dulci Jubilo" by Johann Sebastian Bach on the magnificent 16,000 pipe Hazel Wright Organ. This majestic organ has 287 ranks of pipes. Five thousand pipes are located in the South balcony of the Crystal Cathedral with 549 trumpet pipes located in the East and West balconies, making this one of the largest collections of pipes in the world.

Mark Thallander was a pageant organist for fifteen years playing in more than a thousand pageants. He began his music ministry at the Crystal Cathedral in 1976, four years prior to the first Glory performance. Mark recalled those first few years when the pageants didn't always start on time. Sometimes traffic was backed up with tour buses getting into the parking lot. Mark said, "I would start the prelude on time and then I had to improvise playing Christmas carols—forever and ever—until the cue came for the herald trumpets." Imagine Mark's delight when asked at a staff meeting by Arvella Schuller, "Who was playing those wonderful Christmas carols last night?"

In 1982, Fred Swann began as the Crystal Cathedral's senior organist. The Glory of Christmas was underway. Some of the starting delays had been corrected, and the prelude "In Dulci Jubilo" by J. S. Bach became the official opening for the pageants. During their tenure together, Fred and Mark made a great team in meeting the musical requirements of the ministry. Fred said, "The pageants are a meaningful first class production, not the usual simple church play. They are spiritually oriented and playing for them was a ministry for me to so many people of different faiths from around the world." Fred went on to add, "I knew the score by heart and could concentrate on the delivery."

The organists for the pageants have their own complete score of all of the music and the live organ music is an integral part of the pageant. They play at different intervals and times along with the recorded music by members of the London Symphonic Orchestra and the Seattle Symphony Orchestra. The musical was arranged, orchestrated, and conducted by Johnnie Carl. Mark said, "One Glory of Christmas I played for 60 pageant performances plus Sunday Services." He continued, "During Holy

Week one year, he played for 33 different events including the pageants and special services. I had stacks and stacks of music in different piles to keep organized for that hectic but most significant schedule. On Easter evening, there was a sing along "Messiah" in the Arboretum, and I was finally down to the last pile of music."

The organ console, usually in the center of the Cathedral, is lowered into a pit below the stage and not used during the pageants. A duplicate organ console is located off to one side in the South balcony below a bank of Cathedral windows that can be opened or closed depending on the weather. The windows don't always seal tightly when closed. When the Santa Ana winds blow, air seeps through the windows. Cold air coming from the windows combined with the open doors (for the animals and cast members to enter and exit the show) created several challenges for the organists. Imagine trying to play an organ with cold hands? Both Fred and Mark can remember wearing choir robes over layers of extra clothing to keep warm on some of those nights. They tried to warm their hands during the dramatic scenes so they would be ready to play again for the next musical score.

Secondly, Fred said, "The organ is sensitive to pitch and cold air makes the pitch go down, causing the music to sound off key. It is amusing when the sound technician holds his nose closed." Fred continued, "It is a signal he will cue an audio tape of the organ music at the beginning of the next score." When necessary, they will cover the organ console with a tarp or plastic before a performance to prevent damage to the organ.

Still another challenge occurred the night it rained so hard the windows leaked above the organ console. Mark said, "Someone stood and held an umbrella over me, while I played the organ. We had to keep the music dry and protect the keyboard so rain wouldn't damage the instrument. Both Fred and Mark recall being covered in plastic on some of those rainy nights, until technicians solved a leaky window problem.

For the Glory of Christmas, the set has a massive backdrop that is 140 feet wide by 72 feet high. The set muffles the sound of the organ pipes. It is an opportunity for the organists to use extremely high volume on the organ, which they can't do on a Sunday morning. Mark said, "It is fun adding extra stops to balance with the taped music of London Symphony Orchestra and allow the organ pipes to really fill the Cathedral." Mark chuckled, "It is fine for the audience except I wonder how it affected the people who had to work back stage."

One of the most nerve wracking but also the most delightful time for Mark was playing the trumpet pipes at the beginning of "O Come All Ye

Faithful." He would play the trumpet pipes on the West side of the balcony and alternate with those on the East balcony, as the trumpet pipes echo back and forth. Timing was extremely critical and allowances had to be made for the tremendous distance spanning the Cathedral and any lag time in the sound. Mark said, "I had to think slightly ahead, when I played those keys. It was a challenge, because I wasn't playing soft flutes or strings, but something much more noticeable. I would say a 'Thank you God,' whenever I finished that part."

One evening Mark casually strolled into the Cathedral during the pageant and sat in the West balcony. Mark said, "I never realized how powerful those trumpet pipes are for an audience sitting in the balcony." The trumpet pipes are located above the East and West balconies directly above the angel loft. Having flown as an angel, I assured him we all knew how loud they were. Whenever the trumpet pipes were played, it was a wake up call for the angels to get ready for our last cue. What a joy it was for me to fly over Mark while he played the last flying angel number in the pageant, "Hark, the Herald Angels Sing." Like Fred Swann, he knew the score by memory, and he always sent a sparkling grin my way as I soared overhead.

From time to time Mark would bring one of his organ students to the pageant. He had them sit beside the organ to see the show and watch him play the organ. Their presence heightened Mark's enthusiasm and energy, while playing the same score over and over each night. Mark said, "There is a part in the score when one note sounds a single chime. I would lean over and tell my student about the chime, show him or her the note, and cue them when it came time for them to play it." Mark proudly continued, "My students return years later and tell me what it meant to them to be able to play that one note." Mark admitted, "His students said they told others, they played the organ for the Glory of Christmas at the Crystal Cathedral!"

After eighteen years at the Crystal Cathedral, Mark transferred his organ playing talents to another church. He had established close relationships with the Cathedral staff, members, and volunteers. They wished him well at his new church but were sad to see him go.

In August of 2003, during a summer downpour, his car hydroplaned on a turnpike exit just minutes from his friend, Gary De Vaul's, home in Maine. Mark's left arm was severed in three places. The impact of the accident and seat belt pulled his arm off tearing blood vessels and shredding nerves. Surgeons had no choice but to amputate his left arm.

Word spread and Mark's friends from the Cathedral and the Christian community rose to his aid in prayer. The small hospital caring for him was overwhelmed by the influx of flowers, cards, e-mails, and phone calls conveying positive support. God sent an angel to help rescue Mark at the accident scene and during recovery when death was near. His praying friends, especially Gary De Vaul, became earth angels with their compassionate support during Mark's hospitalization and recovery. Mark's wit and sense of humor amazed Gary. He continued to be amazed at Mark's ability to remain positive after being medicated, only to wake up and say, " I just arranged the hymn "O for a Thousand Tongues to Sing" for one hand and two feet."

Mark enjoys playing the organ. It is his passion. He said, "Playing for the Glory pageants was my evangelistic opportunity. It was a way to let my music speak my faith to reach and touch literally thousands of people." Mark continued, "I have been given a gift to be able play the organ. Even if I was tired or discouraged, I have this gift and few have this kind of opportunity to become involved. I wanted to share my faith by giving my best to each performance."

Mark's positive faith and sense of humor sustained him through his recovery. He possesses a remarkable desire to continue to use the precious musical talents God has given him by continuing to arrange music and perform at churches, concerts, and events with just his two feet and one hand!

*For more information or to contact Mark log on to: www.markthallander.com

Trumpeters' Fanfare

Larry Grossman has played the trumpet in over 2000 Glory of Christmas and Glory of Easter productions. After Johnny Carl heard Larry perform a piccolo/trumpet solo "Rondeau" by Mouret, he was invited to be a trumpeter in the Glory of Christmas pageant. Larry said, "Thanks Johnny" and is still playing in the productions.

There were six trumpeters in the first few years of the Glory of Christmas pageant. Larry said, "We changed clothes a lot." He continued saying, "We had three costume changes. There were costumes for playing as Roman soldiers, shepherds and trumpeters. So we were either playing or changing clothes."

Larry admitted, "It is easier now we have only one costume and eight trumpeters."

Each Glory of Christmas pageant begins for the cast with the stage manager, Sonja Wagner announcing, "Places—all angels, angel operators, spot operators, technicians, organ, trumpets, stage managers and dancers." The special time has come for the pageant to begin. The trumpeter's "Opening Fanfare" stimulates the adrenaline of the cast and audience. The 'follow the star sequence' is the trumpeter's time to play again for "The First Noel" and "Angels We Have Heard On High." Their greatest crescendo and accompaniment is "O Come All Ye Faithful," followed by "Hark, the Herald Angels Sing" and "Joy to the World." Their live musical contribution resonates throughout the Cathedral. The trumpeter's dedication is admirable as they play every night of the pageant.

One night four of the trumpeters played on stage with two in the South balcony for the opening fanfare. When they started playing, one of the sheep got loose and began trotting down the main aisle glancing from side to side. All of a sudden, the sheep jumped up on the stage and snuggled against one of the trumpet player's legs. While the trumpeter was playing, the sheep began rubbing his head up and down against the trumpeter's leg. The trumpeter kept on playing and reached down to push the sheep away. Then the sheep would butt him on the back of the leg.

Larry said, "It was hard to keep from laughing as they continued to keep playing. After all, the trumpeters (and the uninvited sheep) were in the limelight on the center stage."

In the Glory of Easter, the trumpeters have what they call a "rooster fanfare." It takes place just after Jesus is captured in the Garden of Gethsemane and taken to the Sanhedrin court. Jesus' disciples abandon Him. Peter follows the crowd and is watching from the outer courtyard. When approached and asked if he knows Jesus, Peter denies knowing Jesus three times and the rooster crows, "Cock-a-doodle-do!"

The trumpeters' "rooster fanfare" is next. This fanfare is a challenge, since they are spread in three different balconies of the Cathedral. It is also a night scene and dark. They are so far apart, that they can't see each other. They do not have a director. If they did, they couldn't see the person anyway. Starting and stopping in unison is difficult under these conditions. To solve the problem, the trumpeters have Larry lead with a two beat solo, and then all join in on the third beat of the "rooster fanfare." It starts and ends as composed and they take pride in having choreographed the fanfare perfectly.

A similar arrangement was made with Alan Coates*, who plays Pontius Pilate. The trumpeters play a fanfare each time Pilate appears on stage. Alan, as Pilate, was quite creative at interacting with the trumpeters. When awakened from a sound sleep by the tribune he added the word 'Silence' to his script. It was quite effective, but the trumpeters had difficulty stopping at the same time. Someone would always hold a note a little longer than they should. It became a joint collaboration, when

Larry and Alan conversed. Larry learned that Alan had a terrific sense of rhythm. They decided everyone would count 8 beats and then stop. The trumpeters would be able to stop at the same time Pilate (Alan) yells 'Silence!' Imagine the power it gives Pilate, played by Alan, as he silences the trumpets with a single word.

During a rehearsal for the Glory of Easter, eight trumpeters were lined up on the bridge leading to Pontius Pilate's court. Two animal/ trainers were bringing in a live jaguar behind them. The animal/trainers wanted to get the jaguar accustomed to walking the bridge into Pilate's courtyard. One of the animal/trainers led the jaguar by a leash and was pulling him. Another animal/trainer was twisting the jaguar's tail and pushing in an attempt to force him over the bridge. The jaguar kept trying to lie down with each tug. Obviously, the jaguar was not willing to cooperate. The jaguar exercised his instincts by reaching out and locking his front paws around one of the trumpeter's legs. The trumpeter turned a ghostly shade of white. He was not amused. There he was standing on a 20-foot bridge with no place to go and a jaguar holding him by the leg! Fortunately, the jaguar had been de-clawed and the animal/trainers were able to coax the jaguar to release his victim. By the time the show began, the animal/trainers found the jaguar a different way to enter the scene.

Tammy Martz became involved as a trumpet player after attending the pageant. She filled in as a substitute and has now played the trumpet at every performance for eleven years. The Glory's are a family activity for the Martz's. They come every night to the Christmas and Easter shows, since Mom started playing the trumpet. Her husband, Bruce, plays a Roman solder and one of the Three Wiseman. When their daughter Kelly started performing, she ran down the center aisle and jumped into the arms of the singing shepherd. The shepherd's singing must have had a positive musical influence, because Kelly is currently one of the child soloists. Kelly sings "What Can I Give Him" and "Silent Night." The Martz's son, Daniel, is one of the shepherd children. He especially enjoys carrying the baby goats and lambs. Daniel has an amazing grasp of his faith in God, for a nine year old. He told his parents that performing in the show makes him feel he is doing something for the Kingdom of God. His compassion and concern for others is clear with the questions he asks on the way home from pageants.

Daniel asked, "Do the people coming to see the show know about God when they watch us? Do they know what happened to Jesus?

Tammy said, "You can read a passage in the Bible but the pageants bring it to life. That is why our family participates." It is why Tammy joins this dedicated family of trumpeters, who lift audiences up with their fanfares and musical renditions.

Tribute to Johnnie Carl

For almost 30 years, Johnnie Carl conducted the Hour of Power Orchestra at the Crystal Cathedral's Sunday Services. His talents were also sought as the Musical Director/Arranger for the Glory of Christmas and Glory of Easter productions. Through the years, Johnnie's creative musical talents continue to inspire cast members, staff, and audiences attending the pageants.

In the Christmas production, some of Johnnie's compositions include: "Angel Gabriel's Announcement" to Mary informing her that she is to be the mother of the Son of God, Mary's response in the "Magnificat," as well as "Angel Gabriel's" appearance to the shepherds on the hills of Bethlehem. Traditional Christmas music by members of the London Philharmonic Orchestra was added in 1986 under Johnnie's direction, complemented by live music performed on the Cathedral's 16,000-pipe Hazel Wright Organ.

In the Glory of Easter Johnnie composed the triumphant music to "Hosanna," welcoming

Jesus during the Passover week into Jerusalem. He also wrote "Give Thanks to the Lord," performed during the Last Supper that Jesus had with his disciples. Johnnie wrote the "March to Calvary," based on a theme by Dale Wood, along with other arrangements too numerous to mention.

It was not uncommon for cast members in the Glory to find Johnnie, working late at night in his office on a piece of music for another venue. Whenever I walked past his office, Johnnie would stop me for a short chat or we would share a laugh or two. (His favorite laugh was my "surprise angelic landing" on Dr. Robert H. Schuller shown on the cover.) While Maestro Johnnie is no longer conducting music on earth, his creative musical pieces remain and serve as a legacy. Personally, I imagine him composing and conducting music for Heaven's angels as he did for us to enjoy and appreciate on earth.

THE GLORY OF STAGING

Cast & Call

Aundrêa and Alan Wagner were in the third and fifth grades, respectively, at the Crystal Cathedral Academy, when they approached their mother, Sonja Wagner, about being in the Glory of Christmas pageant.

"Please Mom," they begged, "let's sign up to be in the Glory of Christmas pageant." Sonja was an administrative assistant for youth pastor Roger Tirabassi and felt she already had a very busy schedule.

Her children kept insisting, "Everybody else will be doing it." Finally, Sonja gave in and agreed to join them. (A parent or a responsible adult was required to participate with the children.)

Sonja's only condition for joining the cast was, she did not want to be on the main stage. Assistant director Terry Larson, recognizing her concerns, suggested the part of a shepherd. The scenes on the shepherd's hill are night scenes, so she would be less conspicuous than being on center stage. Sonja agreed and during rehearsals everything went smoothly.

On opening night, Sonja was on the hill with other shepherds tending the sheep. Flying angels had returned to their angel lofts. Don Christensen, the shepherd soloist, started singing "While By My Sheep." He walked toward the shepherds standing along the hillside. But on this particular opening night Don paused for a moment and stood beside Sonja. Instantly, the spotlight was upon both of them when the soloist belted out the words "Joy, Joy, Joy" Sonja froze! She stared straight ahead and did not budge. At the end of the scene, her fellow cast members left the hillside, but Sonja remained transfixed, still standing and staring in place.

Finally, a stage manager came and escorted her from the hillside. The stage manager took Sonja to the lower level of the concourse to Room 110. This is the room where the cast gathers throughout the performance waiting for their cues. For Sonja, this room was a safe haven from the spotlight.

It was apparent Sonja would be more comfortable in another role off stage. So she began the task of entertaining the children between their cues in Room 110. Sonja enjoyed playing games and doing arts and crafts projects with them. She did this for several years and then became a stage manager in the East balcony at Christmas and the South balcony at Easter.

These stage manager locations were safe, since she never had to be on stage. She especially liked the South balcony stage manager position, because she could watch the entire show.

"Easter is my passion," Sonja exclaims, "We should celebrate Easter the same way we celebrate Christmas. It provides a greater understanding of the miracle, hope, and joy of the wondrous story of God's love for us."

One evening during the Christmas show, Glenn Grant, as cast manager, had an immediate need for someone to finish calling out the cues for the show. He asked Sonja to fill in and call the places for the cast. Glenn convinced Sonja she could do the job and gave her a quick briefing. So, during the middle of the show, Sonja started calling the cues for the remaining scenes and places over the radio.

At the end of evening, cast members commented, "Sonja, you sounded so good calling our cues." Even the staff agreed and they persuaded her to continue calling cues. She was dubbed the cast and call stage manager—a position she has held the past ten years. (Sonja has participated for seventeen years in the pageants.)

Sonja juggles multiple casting schedules for the volunteers. She enjoys getting acquainted with everyone in the cast, since they all must sign-in at her table when they arrive. Not only does the cast recognize her as the sign-in lady, but they also hear Sonja's voice throughout the lower concourse when she calls their cues. She chuckles when someone signs in after doing a few shows and comments, "Oh, you are the voice we hear all the time."

Cast members share duties and rotate positions for some of the minor roles. Sonja schedules the child or adult who will lead a specific animal in each night. There is a similar schedule for props. It is very important that whoever carries the blue king's seal or the red king's banner knows where to turn and when. This is known as blocking. The individuals responsible for these banners have an entourage of cast members following them. Imagine the chaos if someone made a wrong turn and blocked the procession.

Sign-in time for cast members is critical for Sonja. This is how she determines if the key positions are filled with trained volunteers. She also asks everyone to inform her when a family member or friend is attending. She tries to schedule them to perform on those nights and provides them with a calendar of their scheduled nights and positions. Sometimes, this involves last minute substituting and skill in making those adjustments.

Sonja jokingly told production coordinator,

Sandy Boselo "I think I deserve a degree in psychology by the time the pageants end for all the problems I listen to and the counseling I give them."

Substitutions and 'no shows' are some of Sonja's greatest challenges, requiring split second decisions on her part. During the Glory of Easter, Jesus was taken to Pontius Pilate. Sonja suddenly realized one of the next scenes was the scourging of Jesus. No one had signed-in to do the scourging. She ran down the hall looking for anyone who knew the blocking to do the scene. Her past stage-managing experience came to the forefront. She realized she knew the blocking and could grab a costume. Then her fear of stage fright resurfaced. She quickly calmed her fears, realizing she wouldn't even have to look at the audience. The scene takes place on the center aisle ramp. She would be looking at the stage. The spotlight would be on Jesus and only on her back. So she slipped into the costume, grabbed the whip, and walked onto the ramp.

Jesus, played by Bodie Newcomb*, and a Roman soldier, Eddie Quiroga*, were surprised to see Sonja enter the ramp with the whip. Sonja knew she had to make it appear like she was really hitting Jesus, without actually hurting him. So being short of stature she compensated, but she underestimated her strength as she swung the whip. She saw Bodie, as Jesus, flinch and the look in Eddie's eyes told her she should ease up on the next lashing or disappear after the show. Fortunately, the actor Bodie, like Jesus, was very forgiving, and Sonja was most apologetic.

During another Easter show it was time for the crucifixion. In a few minutes the execution would take place. Three crosses would soon be raised and she was missing a thief. Once again Sonja charged down the halls looking for an appropriate thief. She even went into the men's rest room. For obvious reasons, she knew she could not assume the role this time. All at once, she spotted Matthew Peterson. Now Matthew was a young boy, but also quite tall, in fact, almost 6 feet tall. Instantly, she told Matthew he was going to be a thief and started stripping his clothes. Sonja grabbed a loincloth from Juliet Noriega in the wardrobe department and began going over the thief's lines with Matthew. "You did nothing, save yourself," was all she felt Matthew had time to learn.

The show continued on schedule and Matthew survived his sudden transformation into a thief. However, Robert Winley, in the role of Jesus, was somewhat overwhelmed when he looked over at the second thief and recognized it was a child.

Robert's comment to Sonja after the show

was, "Don't ever put a child on a cross next to me again." This was a true reflection of the compassion, energy, and sensitivity it takes for an actor to perform in the role of Jesus.

Sonja's children, Aundrêa and Alan, have performed various roles through the years. On Children's Day she frantically called her son, Alan. He had just finished working his night job, so he dashed over to the Cathedral in time to play the role of one of the kings. (Children's Day is held during the day for thousands of school children in the area.) Staffing is always more difficult, since many of the volunteers work full time.

For several years, football teams from the high school were given a stipend to be Roman soldiers in the pageant. Sonja coached a girl's softball team. She had some strong looking girls she felt could do the part and the team would benefit from the stipend. The girls willingly volunteered to be Roman soldiers for three years. Nikki and Shannon Resch, from the softball team, remained with the cast longer and their brother, Derek, became an angel operator.

Assisting Sonja with her Cast and Call duties is Sharon Mayer. Things are especially hectic at sign-in time and Sharon helps to keep the flow moving smoothly and quickly. She also serves as a regular cast member, substitutes when someone is missing, and assists with assigning positions for the general cast.

There is a scene in the Glory of Easter where Sharon plays one of the Pharisees ready to stone a young woman caught in the act of adultery. The scribes and Pharisees bring the woman to Jesus saying, "Moses' law commands us that this person should be stoned. But what do You say?"

Jesus stoops down, writes on the ground with his finger, and says, "He who is without sin among you, let him cast the first stone." Sharon along with the Pharisees quickly exit, one by one.

Sharon and Sonja value the friendships they make with all the cast members. "The delightful part," Sonja shared, is observing how being a part of the Glory family has strengthened the faith of my children and some of the young people in the pageants." Sonja continued, "The production is a ministry to the audience, but it is also a ministry to the cast. It helps these young people grow and become mature responsible adults."

Puzzle Pieces

Imagine being responsible for 1200 costume ensembles each containing three to four extra pieces! Juliet Noriega is the wardrobe supervisor and her efficient and energetic assistant is Lisa Goering. At the close of each Glory pageant, all costumes are collected and sent to the dry cleaners. After the costumes are cleaned, they are loaded into twenty-five wardrobe crates and sent to the warehouse for storage.

Two and half weeks before the pageant begins, the general cast begins their rehearsals. Juliet and Lisa arrive to begin the monstrous task of sorting and matching appropriate accessory pieces to each of the costume ensembles. This task is like assembling a giant puzzle. The pieces were separated during the cleaning process and seem to be scattered throughout the twenty-five wardrobe crates. Juliet and Lisa's job is to match the extra belts, ties, scarves, headdresses etc. with the correct costume ensemble.

After a cast member is assigned their part at rehearsal, they proceed to wardrobe to find out which costume they will be checking out and in at performances. Juliet and Lisa are excited as they watch the expressions on the cast members' faces the first time they receive their costumes. Not all costumes are glamorous. The peasant garb during Biblical times was simple and plain, but when the cast members return later and get something to wear for a king's entourage, their faces light up with big smiles.

During rehearsals, fittings take place for outfits that need to be shortened or altered. Sometimes Diana and Sarah Downs help in wardrobe, checking out costumes and serving as dressers. They show the cast how to properly wear and accessorize their costumes. The wardrobe staff also cautions the cast about eating, drinking, and gum chewing while wearing their costumes. Everyone is reminded to handle his or her costume with care. Angel costumes are made of a very delicate fabric and sitting in the costumes is not recommended. During a break between shows, when a meal is served to the cast, large bibs are provided for those who must be in costume for the opening scene.

The costumes were originally designed by Richard Bostard. Richard is involved with all facets of costume design—from the cutting table, to the details of sewing, and dressing. Richard's wardrobe designs have been seen on television in specials for the Public Broadcasting Systems "American Playhouse" and for "Baryshnikov on

Broadway." Many hours of painstaking research went into the costumes for the Glory of Christmas and Glory of Easter to keep them historically authentic in design and fabric. This challenging task gave Richard an opportunity to express extensive creativity. For example, the Roman soldiers wear outfits identical to the legions in the original Roman Army, featuring a short suit of leathered armor covered with bronze. Even the helmets are authentic with large shakos extending from the top to the back of the helmets.

During the off-season, Juliet refurbishes and repairs costumes for the next show. Once again, she is working on a puzzle of various costume pattern pieces. Sometimes she only replaces a part of the costume, while other times she remakes the entire costume. Juliet has all the original patterns. Her goal is to maintain the original design and appearance of every costume. This tedious work includes adhering to the quality, flavor, feel, and texture of the fabrics. With all the new fabrics on the market, selection is a monumental task.

Juliet admits she enjoys buying the fabrics and making the costumes. In order to make one of the kings' robes, she starts with a king sized quilted bedspread. A few years ago, she was backpacking and hiking in Morocco. She couldn't resist the fabric stores and admitted, "I found this piece of absolutely gorgeous electric blue Moroccan fabric that I knew would be perfect for the blue kings robe. So I bought it." Juliet chuckled as she continued, "That was at the beginning of my trip. I had to carry all this extra Moroccan fabric in my backpack during the rest of my trip!" It is this kind of commitment and dedication that continues to sustain the overall quality of these pageants. Perhaps Juliet has forgotten about her heavy backpack, until she sees the Blue King ride on stage wearing an elegant Moroccan robe draped over the hump of his dromedary camel.

There have been some challenging, panicky moments for the wardrobe team. A cast member in costume "gets animaled," (a kind description for animal excretions) and a quick costume change is required.

Juliet recalls the year she made a fabulously elegant gold robe for the gold king. (King Melchoir) It was the night before Children's Day, so it was early in the show season. They had a photo shoot that evening. After the photo, the gold king's robe somehow got caught on a nail, while he was riding his camel. The gold robe was completely ripped in half. At first, it was heart wrenching for Juliet, since the new robe was only in the show for a week. But with Children's Day the next morning, she went at 6:00 AM to the warehouse to pick up another gold robe.

Wardrobe keeps duplicates of every costume for these unexpected circumstances. Dry cleaning is sent out regularly during the shows, while some things can be machine-washed. Repairs are on going during all of the shows.

Joel Miller was the wardrobe supervisor in 1984, when Juliet joined the wardrobe team. Juliet assisted Joel for six years and returned in 1994 as the wardrobe supervisor. Juliet said, "I have seen children return as adults. It has been an evolutionary process in how I relate to people. I am exposed to people of all ages, backgrounds, and personalities, some more spiritual than others."

Juliet continued, "It has been exciting to watch the cast members grow and change through the years. It is like a human evolution for me and for them. At first it was a job, but now I relate to them differently than I once did. I find myself looking deeper into their needs and their joys." Like assembling the pieces of a puzzle, Juliet enjoys returning each year to see which piece in the cast has grown and changed.

Homespun Props

Sets + Wigs + Make-up

In most theatrical shows, the properties (props) department is a separate department. It is very unusual to combine the three departments—properties, set decor, wigs and make-up under one umbrella with one manager. Sharon Crabtree* is a designer and member of the Screen Actors Guild and the Actors Equity Association. She has successfully managed these three departments in the Glory of Christmas and Easter for the past twenty years. Sharon is quick to acknowledge her team of assistants, Linda Booher, Fred Booher and Michael Adkins for their combined efforts in helping to make everything operate smoothly.

Prior to working with props, Fred Booher wore a Roman soldier's costume in the pageants. He was the Captain of the Guard at Christmas and a sentry at Easter. Linda Booher was the wine lady. Since Linda's jug was brown in color, inside and out, she would comment jokingly, "Look at my chocolate wine!" The following year

Linda became a stage manager. She enjoyed teaching new cast members their roles and assuring them that they would know their parts before curtain time.

The Boohers' daughters also joined the cast. Kelly was a flying angel for several years, while Kasey, an animal lover, preferred leading animals on stage. Linda's next adventure was helping Sharon Crabtree* in the props department. Linda has been a member of the Crystal Cathedral congregation since she was seven years old, and has been involved with the pageants for eighteen years.

From food baskets to wine jugs, spears to shields, from items as tiny as coins to as large as an 8 foot cross; these are just a few of the props used in the pageants. There are over 150 different props in the Glory of Christmas and in the Glory of Easter. Sharon researches each prop and set design for its Biblical authenticity. Tremendous care is given to using natural fabrics, bamboo, leather, twines, raffia, and gourds. All of these items are similar to what would have been available 2000 years ago in the Holy Land. The sets and props are built to be beautiful up close, so the audience can appreciate their intricate patterns and design. Sharon is especially pleased with the elegance of the grail (cup or chalice) used during the Lord's Supper.

Sharon said, "The grail is hand blown glass and signed by the artist. When light touches the grail, it gleams like a jewel."

She went on to say, "The audience is moved by the writing and the acting, but they are also touched by the visual details of the pageant. People come to these pageants because they are deeply affected by what they see."

The Boohers' home serves as headquarters for the reconditioning and building of some of the props. Linda and Fred's backyard is perfect for drying the palm branches used in the Glory of Easter production. One year Sharon purchased and gathered the palm branches from a farm, which had just finished trimming their date palm trees. The palms fronds are cut to size and the points are removed. The stems are wrapped with tape before drying. After the palm fronds dry, they are painted green to look fresh. If more fresh palm branches are needed, the entire process takes about a month. Otherwise, Sharon's team just repaints the palm fronds each year to make them look fresh again.

At the close of each production, Sharon determines what props or sets need to be refurbished or replaced. If it is a major project, it will begin during the off-season. One year, the large banners carried by the wise men's entourage were updated. Fabric was replaced; jewels and fringe were added for a more elegant appearance. Another year, Sharon chose to replace the seven tents used in the Glory of Easter. Again, she bought fabric and her teams combined efforts accomplished the task. Imagine cutting, assembling and sewing seven large tents! The Boohers' home had pieces of fabric and an assembly line process going on in every room of their house. Their family members were crawling over and under numerous tents in various stages of completion while carrying on normal daily living.

On the Thursday before the cast begins rehearsals, cages with stored props arrive from the warehouse. Sharon and her team unpack the cages and repair any props or sets as needed. They lay various props on tables in sequence for each scene. The team inspects the props and directs cast members in the best ways to handle the props. It is essential the cast member understand, for example, how to carry a large basket of fruit so the fruit is visible to the audience, but also in a way so the fruit won't dangle or fall out.

At the beginning of each scene, they verify the location of essential props, (such as the hammer and nails for the crucifixion). If a needed prop is still visible in the prop room, they radio a stage manager who will designate a cast member to come get it. Sharon's team also checks props back in, verifying good condition of all props and repairing any damage before the next performance. With multiple performances a night, successful presentations require strict attention to detail and proper procedures are crucial.

In the Glory of Easter, the disciples prepare to meet Jesus in the upper room to celebrate their Last Supper together. The table used for the Lord's Supper is on a hydraulic lift under the floor of the stage. It is usually raised during a darkened scene as the disciples gather around to begin the celebration. On one particular evening the table didn't rise and the disciples were still standing around.

Immediately, the stage manager made a desperate radio call, "The table didn't come up. We need the bread and wine." Linda heard the radio message and immediately grabbed an extra communion set. She darted out of the prop room, up the stairs, and handed it to one of the disciples standing at the East edge of the stage. Realizing the problem, some of the disciples had already improvised and began sitting down at different levels on the steps of the set. A disciple handed Jesus the jug of wine and the bread. Jesus proceeded with the breaking of bread and the pouring of the wine. The disciples teasingly dubbed it, "The Lord's Supper Picnic!"

Another year during the crucifixion, the sponge Jesus is given fell behind a piece of the set. A stage manager radioed the prop room and Linda quickly dashed up the stairs. She slipped behind the set with another sponge and handed it to a cast member on stage. For obvious reasons, there are duplicate sets of key props for these interesting and unexpected circumstances.

Sharon styles the wigs and applies the make-up worn by the Three Kings at Christmas and for Jesus at Easter. Sharon stays late, after the show ends each night, to clean the wigs worn by the actors each evening. Michael Adkins, her dedicated volunteer, stays to assist. Everyone else has left and the Cathedral is empty and dark. Sharon has high praise for Michael regarding his commitment. He gets up at 4:00 AM to go to work and then stays until she finishes the wigs, so he can escort her to the parking lot. Sharon and Michael are the very last ones to leave the Cathedral. Their cars are the last cars in the parking lot.

During the final show, the properties team begins packing some of the props. Each item is wrapped in plastic or bagged. Special crates are designed to protect fragile items like the chalice and Wiseman gifts. The crates and bagged items are placed in one of a dozen designated 6-foot metal cages. The following Monday after the show ends, Sharon's team returns to complete the packing process. The cages are taken to the warehouse and stored until next year's production begins.

Child Wrangler

It's not every theater production that creates a need for an Off-Stage Children's Stage Manger. However, when up to 35 children are involved in the cast with long waits between cues, boundless energy erupts.

As the Assistant Director, Terry Larson was on a first name basis with nearly everyone associated or involved with the Glory productions. Terry provided the glue and grease for everything to run smoothly. He was perceptive had a way of finding creative solutions to any challenge with a beneficial outcome for everyone involved in the production.

Young children have always been a part of the pageants. Entire families participated. But there were times when parents were on stage or supporting in other areas, while their children were waiting downstairs in the Cathedral with other cast members until their cues were called. When mom and dad are out of sight, you know what can happen. Some children became anxious, others were bored while waiting. Those long hallways under the sanctuary were beckoning some boys and girls to try various running games. Terry recognized that something needed to be done. He approached Kelly Williamson with a proposal that she become the Off-Stage Children's Stage Manager (Child Wrangler). Kelly's two sons, Kyle and Cory, wanted to be in the pageant. This was the perfect opportunity for their family to become involved as a team.

The Official Toy Cabinet was initially provided with colors and puzzles. During the seven years their family participated, Kelly added games, books, and even videos. Their favorite game was Mancala, an African bead game. Kelly had to stay sharp playing with the young actors because they loved changing the rules without her knowledge.

Kelly's main job was to be sure the children had their costumes on correctly and met their cue calls. The children especially liked the scenes where they were responsible for leading a goat or sheep on and off the stage and then returning them to their tie-down spots. For those who did not have pets at home, it was like owning a pet for a short time. The children became quite attached and even gave them pet names. A baby lamb born on Christmas Eve was affectionately named, Glory.

Performance times varied depending on the day of the week and time of year. Sometimes there were two to three performances an evening. (I recall flying as an angel in four shows a night the weekends near Christmas.) At the close of each performance, when the audience exits the Cathedral from the east and west balconies, they are greeted by the barnyard smells of hay and animals outside the balcony entrance. Sometimes, the children will be standing close by and petting their special animal, grinning proudly, as if to claim ownership.

Repositioning the camels for the next performance was the trainers' responsibility. Here was one of the fringe benefits for Kyle, of having a mom as a stage manager. Kyle and his mom were able to ride a King's camel to re-position it outside from the east to the west balcony to get ready for the next show. Imagine telling your grade school friends about what it is like to ride at least 6 feet in the air on a single-humped Dromedary camel.

Children's Day is a special event. It is one of the most exciting and busiest days at the Cathedral for the cast. On this day 20,000 school children from the local area are bused in for one of six daytime performances. At one of these performances, a newborn black lamb got loose and was jumping and spraying across the stage, "baa . . . ing" as loud as his little nostrils would permit with each leap. Even more amusing, especially to the children in the cast, the lamb was prancing up and down in the wrong direction across the stage. The incident became the main topic of discussion, a vivid lesson on the importance of paying close attention when herding your animal.

Homework was the first consideration when the children arrived before a performance. Each child, who had homework, must complete it before getting anything from the Official Toy Cabinet. During the Easter show, little Shannon arrived with some vocabulary homework. The teacher had informed Shannon's class that a grown-up had to do the vocabulary work with them and sign off on the homework form. So Kelly and Shannon did the homework together and when they finished Shannon said, "I need you to sign here, 'cause you were the one to help me to do this."

"OK," Kelly replied and she signed on the line.

The next evening when Shannon arrived, she looked very unhappy and sad. Kelly asked, "Shannon, what's wrong?"

"I didn't get credit for my homework," Shannon lamented.

"Why not?" Kelly asked.

"The teacher can't read your squiggly signature. She doesn't think you are a grown-up," Shannon timidly replied. Very slowly and with emphasis Shannon went on to say "She wants you to Print Your Name!"

Kelly couldn't help but chuckle at her own shortcomings and immediately assured Shannon she would correct the situation with the teacher, so she would get credit. It was in that moment Kelly realized that God had given her many talents, but handwriting was not one of them.

THE GLORY of
A FAMILY
AFFAIR

A Family Affair

Don & Trudy Miller Family
An answer to prayer for Don & Trudy Miller
25 years of "Glory" participation

In October of 1980, at a Sunday morning Crystal Cathedral church service, Trudy and Don Miller were reading in the Sunday bulletin about the Cathedral's plan to produce a play called the Glory of Christmas. The bulletin included a request for volunteer cast members to make it happen. Previously, the Millers had been praying for guidance regarding their involvement in the church. They wanted to do something together as a family. The invitation was an immediate signal for both of them to volunteer. As with most undertakings, there was some discussion about the time commitment it would take at such a busy time of year for their family. Recalling Matthew 19:26, "With God all things are possible," they realized the key was making the commitment and all the rest would follow.

The month of rehearsals was wonderful,

interesting and exciting for Trudy and Don. The Christmas season took on new meaning when they were given specific names for the characters they were to portray. Trudy and Don felt they were actually living the First Christmas. They were the characters wearing the costumes of the day, living the history, reading the Bible. The Millers' hearts were filled with joy and blessings to be part of the cast as they shared their faith and developed new friendships within their Glory Family. Trudy and Don were so inspired that they made a family commitment to continue to participate in the Glorys and created their own family prayer. "We are so blessed being a blessing. Thank You, God. Amen."

Don was dedicated to his family, his work and the Glory productions. After completing his job as the engineering construction manager on the Newport Center project for the Irvine Company, Don went to work for Continental Development in Manhattan Beach. As a condition of his employment, Don stated he would only take the job if he could continue to be a cast member in the Glory pageants. His family's commitment and dedication became a ministry to his co-workers as he showed them videos of the pageants and/or helped arrange for them to buy tickets.

It was at a 4th of July family weekend at Lake Tahoe that Don experienced severe neck pains, only to learn later that cancer had already spread throughout his body. The initial diagnosis was that Don had six months to live, but he and his family were blessed with almost five more years of togetherness. They continued to participate in the Glory productions and found strength and prayerful support in the bonding that took place within the cast of their Glory Family.

The Glory's have been a joyous "Family Affair" for Trudy and Don Miller. Their children joined them whenever possible and son, Kevin, is still involved as one of the Three Kings at Christmas or as one of Jesus' Disciples at Easter. Grandsons, Ian and Aaron Daly, are also involved in the cast as Roman soldiers or shepherds. Don participated for 15 years, but it is Trudy who deserves a "Halo" as she has been in every Glory of Christmas and Easter for the past 25 years. This makes her the longest serving Glory Volunteer!

Trudy has portrayed almost every female character in the scripts, from the entourage to the shepherd lady, the Innkeeper's wife to the Blind Man's mother with humility and gratefulness to be a part of the volunteer cast. She is a living example of her Family's Prayer, "We are so blessed being a blessing, Thank You, God. Amen."

The Miller Family, like many individuals and

families who have donated their time, feel privileged to be a part of the cast. At the close of each performance, cast members in costume gather outside to greet the audience. Great joy and inspiration comes from this interaction with the audience. They are touched by the beautiful comments from people around the world who have come for the pageants. For the audience, it is a memorable photo opportunity to stand next to someone in costume and be a part of that time and place in history. For Trudy Miller, it is the realization that each performance of the Glory of Christmas or the Glory of Easter brings each of us closer to God and that is the purpose.

A Family Affair

Jim & Connie Downs Family

20 Years of "Glory" Participation

In 1984 Jim and Connie Downs were not attending a church, but Connie felt it was important for their children to be spiritually grounded. So they bused the children to local Sunday schools in Ontario, California where they lived. Soon after, they started watching the "Hour of Power" on television. Later, a friend invited them to attend an Easter Sunday Service at the Crystal Cathedral. Connie was impressed.

The first time the Downs Family came after that Easter Service, they sat in the East balcony. A white haired usher by the name of Carl Treen greeted their family and asked, "Hi how are you? Are you folks new?"

"Yes, we are," Jim replied.

"Where are you folks from?" Carl asked.

"Ontario, California" responded Jim.

"What are your names?" Carl asked.

"Jim and Connie Downs." Jim replied.

"Well, I'm Carl, says so, right here on my badge." Carl went on to say, "Welcome to the Crystal Cathedral." Carl's friendly manner made them feel welcome.

The next Sunday, when the Downs family returned to the Cathedral, Carl greeted them and asked, " Hi Connie, hi Jim, how are you doing? How was the trip down from Ontario?" This time it was Jim who was impressed. Their family continued coming to the Cathedral the rest of the summer. The children went to Sunday school and Jim and Connie always sat in the East balcony, where Carl ushered.

In the fall of that same year, 1984, Jim and Connie joined the Crystal Cathedral congregation. Carl Treen's personal attention as an usher made an impact. Jim and Connie volunteered to usher for the Glory of Christmas. In those days an interview with Bill Carr, Joe Pardini, Robert Garrett, and Norman Tuck was necessary prior to ushering.

Jim commented, "They wanted to be sure our hearts were in the right place, I guess. Besides, this committee required a commitment of ten nights of ushering." Jim and Connie were assigned to the West balcony and after three nights of ushering Jim was having a ball. He went over to the head usher and said, "Hey, Bill if you need me for more nights, I am available." His offer was accepted!

A few months later, when the Glory of Easter began, Jim and Connie were eager to continue ushering. Sarah, their daughter, joined them for the pageant and was cast as Jarius' daughter. The first scene of the Glory of Easter opens with Jarius and his family weeping at the death of their daughter. Sarah, as the dead daughter, is lying on a raised platform. (Sarah is the first person to play the part of the dead girl in the Easter pageant.)

Sonja Wagner, the downstairs cast and call stage manager, gives the cues for the show. Members of the cast, waiting in the lower concourse, hear Sonja's announcements for cues and places. "Dead girl scene. Places, dead girl's family. Places, dead girl's sister," Sonja calls.

Possibly it was the cue call that influenced Sarah's friends to introduce her by saying," You have to meet Sarah, she's the first dead girl!" A few years later when Sarah went to help in the wardrobe shop, girls would still refer to Sarah as the "first dead girl."

Her first year in the Glory of Easter, Sarah was in another scene leading up to the Crucifixion. It is during the time when Pilate commands that Jesus be scourged, hoping the flogging will satisfy the hostile crowd. The crowd continues to insist that Jesus be crucified. Pilate remains hesitant, realizing he cannot find anything Jesus has done wrong. Then Pilate presents a compromise to the crowd. During each Passover, it is a custom for the Romans to release one condemned man. Pilate offers the crowd two choices and says, "I ask again, shall I release the murderer Barrabas or Jesus, King of the Jews."

The angry crowd yells, "Release Barrabas! Release Barrabas!"

Then Pilate turns to Jesus and asks the crowd, "What shall I do with this man?"

The crowd replies again, "Crucify Him!"

Sarah is part of the crowd that wants Jesus released. So Sarah runs and jumps into the arms of one of the Roman soldiers, named Vitelius. She leans over into his microphone and in her little girl voice says, "Please don't kill him."

At the beginning of each production, another member of the Down's Family would turn nine. (Nine was the minimum age to be in the pageant.) The Downs children brought along neighborhood friends, so they always had a car full of lively volunteers. One Easter Robbie brought his friends, Terry Parker and Mauro Estrada.

During the Glory of Easter show, Robbie and his friends were among the crowd in the temple square. They observed the moneychangers selling their wares. A blind man was sitting by the pool of Siloam. Jesus was seated teaching a small group of people on the temple steps. Being typical young boys full of mischief, Robbie and his friend Terry had an idea. They would steal from the rich and give to the poor, like Robin Hood. Without any hesitation, they acted on their idea. Terry distracted the moneychangers. Robbie ran across the stage, grabbed some money, and gave it to the blind man waiting by the pool of Siloam. The producer, Paul David Dunn, and the directors liked the boys' idea and made it a part of the show. They even added a slight twist by having one of the Roman soldiers call Robbie a "thief" and chase after him.

During his teen years, Robbie's knack for running on stage placed him in the role of the scribe. At Christmas, he was a scribe in King Herod's Court and at Easter he was also a scribe delivering messages to Pilate. Robbie would run on stage saying "A message from Caiaphas. A message from Caiaphas with his seal!" and run off again.

Robbie's next big role was during Crucifixion scene. He was the second thief on the cross who turned to Jesus and asked, "Jesus, remember me when You come into Your kingdom." Robbie's dad Jim, teased him about that role and said, "See your life crime — stealing from the moneychangers in the temple caught up with you." (For more about Robbie's involvement in the Glory see the story "A Disciple's Audition.)

What fascinated Jim and Connie were their children's reactions to the characters they played, and the resulting relationships they developed with other cast members. For Jim and Connie, it was an amazing opportunity to see God working in their children's lives. This was especially obvious the first year their young daughter Diana was in the Glory of Easter.

Diana was a tiny little nine year old, content to be part of the various crowd scenes. It was clear to Connie that Diana was intrigued with the person playing the role of Jesus, namely Robert Miller. Like Jesus, Robert was thirty-three years old and a carpenter by trade. Diana would watch Robert's every move as Jesus. She would wait patiently by the East exit for him to come down from performing in the ascension scene. Jesus, (Robert) would take Diana's little hand and together they would walk side-by-side down the stairs to the concourse level. Diana's glowing face reflected her thoughts. In that moment, Diana was actually holding Jesus' hand and walking with Him. For Connie, seeing the joy in her daughter's eyes showed the glorious way God was at work in her daughter's life.

Connie admits, "Children have an amazing

vision. They don't see the difference between reality and fantasy, which is sometimes difficult for grown-ups to experience. Most adults would have just seen a man in the role of Jesus. But to Diana, this man was Jesus!"

Connie enjoyed watching her children in various roles in the pageants, but she herself was also involved as a stage manager. At first, she was a bit overwhelmed having never had any theater experience. But she spent time observing the professional stage managers and learning from them. Connie established two key concepts that she determined were necessary, besides prayer, to meet the needs of cast members in her section of the stage.

1. Make certain the cast was prepared in every way so God could use them effectively. Make sure all participants knew where they were supposed to be and when. Check to see if they had the right props, the full instructions for handling and placement of all props.

2. Encourage the cast members to be open to receive all they in turn would give to the audience. After all, they were going to be "the living presentation of the Gospel message."

Stage-managing was filled with challenges and a multitude of joys for Connie. She felt her role was to be a cast member's cheerleader or crying towel, whatever they needed to help them portray God's message to the audience.

Working with volunteers required additional adjustments. There were constant nightly changes with volunteer cast members. At Christmas, the run of the show is longer. (Run of the show means the number of shows scheduled and repeated in a certain time frame.) There are two casts at Christmas. They are known as the red cast and the green cast. At Easter, the show has a shorter run and there is only one general cast. Sometimes the volunteers in these casts have personal obligations and can't come on their scheduled night. When someone else substitutes or doesn't show up at the last minute, the stage manager has to quickly brief another volunteer on the part to be filled.

Many of the volunteers are arriving directly from their daytime jobs or family responsibilities. Often the stage manager has less than five minutes for instruction. This includes explaining their point of entry, and the fastest way to reach it in time for their cue. This briefing includes which props they need, and what to do with the props. It is especially critical when someone uses a prop that is also being used in a later scene. Laura (LaLa) Martinez is part of the crowd scene, where Jesus is whipped when standing before Pontius Pilate. After the scene ends, it is Laura's responsibility to take the whip, slip quietly off-stage, and position the whip so it will be available for a later scene.

Imagine the panic that occurred one evening when Jesus was to enter the scene carrying the cross on the way to Calvary to be crucified, and the cross had not been re-positioned. Incidents like this make stage-managing a predominately volunteer cast even more challenging. Adding animals to numerous scenes requires even more endurance, creativity, and patience. Whether managing people or animals, the stage managers recognize similarities. People and animals are sometimes alike; both can be unpredictable!

When Connie and Jim's daughter, Diana was younger she was part of the general cast in different crowd scenes. As a teenager, Diana enjoyed volunteering in wardrobe. The first year, her supervisor was Joel Miller. The following year, Juliet Noregia was in charge assisted by Lisa Goering. The wardrobe duties varied. Diana would help check out costumes to the cast members when they arrived and check the costumes back in upon their return at the end of a scene. She even helped dress some cast members requiring quick changes.

Keeping things sanitary was important, especially with animals constantly around the cast. When the sandals were returned, they would need sanitizing with alcohol. One of

Diana's jobs was to spray each pair of sandals with alcohol. Volunteering in wardrobe allows interaction with each of the cast members and is a friendly place to be involved.

The Downs youngest son, Jimmy, eventually joined the cast as a Roman soldier. Something about wearing armor appeals to young boys. Things became even more appealing when Jimmy started ushering in one of the balconies. It seems there was a young lady also ushering in the same balcony. Could that have been the reason?

Numerous romances started to bud or bloom during participation in the pageants. Some died off but some reappeared. It may have taken them a decade, but eventually a former Cathedral, security guard, Tony Van Dyke and flying angel, Debbie Zubiate were married and celebrated their wedding at a reception in Laguna, California.

Jim and Connie Downs know their family's involvement in the Glory productions had a positive impact on their children and led each of them to a deeper faith and relationship with the Lord. Through the years, some members of their family have moved out of the area, while others are still involved.

Participation in the pageants was also an opportunity for the Downs' Family to examine their faith. Connie said, "The pageants give our family a chance to celebrate the birth and life of Jesus in a unique and wonderful way. God is real. You can reach out and touch Him. You can dance at the feet of the Newborn Christ, ride a camel, or escort in a King! You have an opportunity to take in the message night after night, year after year.

Connie continued, "There is a feeling of satisfaction by being involved. It is a joy. You say to yourself 'I get to do this!' We never felt it was a sacrifice. We always felt if we missed out on doing the pageants, we were going to miss out on something great." So it was natural for Jim to continue as Head Usher/Special Events Coordinator with the newest pageant, the summer production of "Creation."

A Family Affair

Fred & Sandy Asche Family

Fred and Sandy Asche have four daughters, Stephanie, Emily, Angel, and Tiffany who were involved in the Glory of Christmas and Glory of Easter for twelve consecutive years. Tiffany was the youngest daughter. She and Dad had date nights, until she turned nine and could participate in the pageants. Prior to her participating in the Glory, they would color, play games and even go for Tiffany's favorites, hotdogs and ice cream.

Each evening, Glory performances begin with a cast prayer and a short Biblical or related story. Prayer times were led by various pastors from the Cathedral, cast members, or selected volunteers. From time to time, Fred Asche, head of the Asche Family, would lead the cast prayers. The rest of his family were more involved in the pageants with different roles to play requiring a greater commitment of time.

Daughter Emily had some interesting experiences with the animals. She recalls the night during the journey to Bethlehem, when the billy goat butted her in the back. She rolled head over heels and literally summer-saulted down the ramp into the center aisle. She was worried the audience might have seen her tumble and be afraid that she was hurt. A bit stunned at first, she shook her head, stood up, frowned at the goat, grabbed his leash, and led him down the ramp and back behind the curtain.

Another time, when she was standing near the manger, a cow stepped on her foot and broke it. That challenge didn't stop Emily either. She just hobbled in and continued playing her part during the next few weeks of performances.

Emily's greatest challenge with animals came when she was tending a flock of geese in the Easter pageant. Emily and the geese had been corralled in a kiosk at the main entrance of the Cathedral waiting for their cue. Some of the ushers were chosen to help Emily by lining up side by side to create an aisle from the kiosk to the center ramp. When the cue finally came, the geese would not move. The creative ushers sensed the urgency of the situation. The ushers started flapping their black coat jackets open and closed to get the geese moving from the kiosk up the center ramp. Emily and her friend tried using sticks to keep the waddling geese together, as they began to herd them down the center aisle. The geese, however, started flapping their wings and honking loudly, drowning out the music. Then the geese tried to fly. (Fortunately, their wings had been clipped.) Emily finally managed to herd them, still honking, toward the east exit.

Once outside, the geese sensed freedom and started running about the campus and jumping into the reflecting ponds. Emily went chasing after them determined to catch those critters. She slipped off her sandals, waded into a pool, reached out, and grabbed the goose by the neck. She managed to capture all three geese, while her friend stood by and watched.

When she got home that evening she announced to her father, "Tonight I learned how to catch a goose!" (The geese performed for two shows but are no longer a part of the live animal cast.)

Sandy, Emily's mother, was raised on a farm and often wondered if her daughters would ever learn what it meant to care for animals. The pageants provided a special opportunity for them to have those experiences.

In the opening scene of the Glory of Easter, Jesus approaches the family of Jarius. The family is weeping and wailing over the death of their daughter. Sandy Asche is playing the part of the dead girl's mother. Angel, her real life daughter, is playing the part of Jarius's daughter. The girl had been dead for three days. In that moment, Sandy felt an emotional loss surging through her body of what it must mean to lose a child.

"Why are you weeping?" asked Jesus. "Don't be afraid. The child is not dead, she is only sleeping." As He knelt over the child and gave thanks, Jesus said, "Little Girl, little girl, I say to you, Arise!" It was an incomprehensible feeling for Sandy to experience both sadness and joy as her very own daughter, Angel, jumped up and ran into her arms.

Angel played the role of an incense bearer at Christmas. She wore an intricately beaded blue and silver headdress, while she was part of King Balthazar's entourage. She was kneeling with the rest of the entourage at the manger during a "freeze scene." (A time when no humans or animals in the group were to move.) The manger angel, Susan Tillou, was flying overhead to the music of "Hark, the Herald Angels Sing." Being quiet and motionless was not an option for a baby goat. He was hungry and was attracted to Angel's headdress. Knowing she wasn't supposed to move, Angel sat perfectly still, while the baby goat started nibbling at her lovely hairpiece. He kept nibbling and nibbling as Angel remained motionless. By the end of the scene, the baby goat had eaten a hole completely through the wonderful headdress. At the next performance, there was one less headdress and one very tired, but full, baby goat.

Cast members were encouraged to talk to one another during some of the scenes, and to take on the role of the character they were portraying. Sandy was quick to make it realistic. During one scene, she was walking with her three daughters on their journey to Bethlehem. When another traveler stopped them and asked about her husband, Sandy replied, "Some wolves killed him on the hills of Judea." She was so sincere they believed her real life husband had actually been killed.

During the Glory of Easter, the children brought Sandy artificial flowers that resembled lotus blossoms. Sandy and the children pretended to use the lotus blossoms to make a perfume ointment. Debby Smith Tebay, as Mary Magdalene, stopped to buy the perfume. This perfume was used later to wash Jesus' feet. Debby shared with Sandy and the children, "In Biblical times, the cost of this small bottle of perfume would have been equivalent to a year's wages." Comments like this between cast members, who had researched their characters, made participation in the pageants even more meaningful.

The Asche family truly enjoyed being the

shepherds and tending the sheep. It was even more rewarding for Sandy, when she could lend a steady arm to Shepherd Gary Franken. Gary had cerebral palsy and usually was wheel chair bound. Gary was also a helpful teammate to serve as Sandy's escort in the darker scenes on the way to the shepherds' fields. Sandy provided Gary the arm he needed for balance. Gary, who worked for Cal Trans during the day spotting road hazards, provided the eyes for them to see during these darker scenes. Gary pointed out the marble-sized sheep droppings they needed to avoid during their walk up shepherds' hills. When stepped on and squished between the toes of their sandals, these sheep droppings were definitely considered a road hazard. (A challenge every cast member, especially the dancers, tried to avoid both on and off stage.)

Sandy and her daughter, Stephanie, shared a special time flying together as angels in the Glory of Easter. After 6 weeks of rehearsals and 90 minutes of waiting in the east balcony for their cue, the time came for them to be hooked up to the #2 and #3 angel wire positions. They were the first pair of mother/daughter flying angels. After their angel pilots checked and rechecked the wire fittings, they were hoisted up and suspended in the darkness waiting for their cue. Before every angel flight, they would reach out as far as they could toward one another and just barely touch with their fingertips. This fingertip touch became a prayer between them. They would ask the Lord to have them do what He wanted of them and to bless everyone attending the pageant.

Flying as an angel was a meaningful spiritual experience for Sandy, as it was for many of us who have flown as angels. Sandy recalled one very intense evening after the earthquake scene followed by the resurrection. She was suspended in darkness, suddenly feeling as if the wires weren't there.

Sandy said, "I was simply floating in air without being connected to any type of flying apparatus. I saw the Risen Christ in all His Glory. It was one of the most remarkable times of my life. I was soaring above the audience with their 'upturned faces' announcing the glorious news "Christ the Lord has Risen Today." To announce Christ's resurrection to those 'upturned faces' was as though I was dispensing God's blessings upon them. Everyone has challenges, problems, and some are struggling with an ignorance of Christianity or unbelief."

Sandy continued, "The upturned face was the Lord's way of using flying angels, to pour out His blessings on them. It was like watering flowers in a flower garden, so they would grow spiritually and continue thrive in the blessings He provides."

THE GLORY OF
CHOREOGRAPHY

Heavenly Hosts

Mary Martin, the actress who flew in the Broadway production of Peter Pan, suggested to Dr. Robert H. Schuller, that he should have flying angels in the Glory of Christmas pageant. Mary Martin introduced Dr Schuller to "Flying by Foy," a company well known in the industry for their theatrical flying endeavors. Peter Foy flew Mary Martin and proceeded to make flying angels a possibility in the Crystal Cathedral.

Dorie Lee Matteson was the choreographer for the Glory of Christmas and became the first Flying Angel Gabriel in the Glory of Christmas. She was launched from a raised platform located on the landing of the West balcony in full view of the balcony audience. It was assumed the audience would be so engrossed in what was happening on stage, they wouldn't be watching the angel pilots as they prepared to launch an angel. Dorie flew from a wire attached to a track in the ceiling from the West to the East balcony. Gayle

Carter Carline was one of three other angels flown on stage. These angels were lifted in a vertical up and down position from behind the wooden stable used for a manger.

Numerous adjustments were made to the placement of angel tracks in the years that followed. Dorie flew from various locations on stage and from the balconies. Gayle joined her in these attempts to perfect the flying aspects of the show. The angels wear harnesses under their costumes and some were designed for only a single wire.

One of the first scripts had an angel landing on stage. The single wire made it more difficult for Tony Elevi, Peter Foy's flying supervisor, to land Dorie given the way the set was designed. The second drawback was that the angels kept turning on a single wire. When Susan Tillou was flying as the Angel Gabriel, instead of facing the Virgin Mary during the annunciation, she kept turning and therefore sometimes Angel Gabriel, (Susan) would have her back to the Virgin Mary. Finally, it was decided to fly all of the angels from harnesses equipped with attachments for two wires. This kept them from turning. One season an angel flew from the South balcony, but since then eight angels fly for the Glory of Christmas and six fly for the Glory of Easter.

Angel auditions are held twice a year, in September and February prior to the dancer auditions. Laura Martinez (La La) was in church the Sunday I was interviewed as a flying angel on the Hour of Power. Her husband Nick said, "You could be an angel and do what Venna does. Why don't you try out when they have auditions?"

Laura (La La) replied, "Do you really think so?" She recalled all those ballet lessons she had as a child and wondered if this wasn't the time to reap the benefits of those lessons.

Nick replied, "They just announced auditions for the Glory of Easter in February."

When February arrived, Laura (La La) went to the auditions. I had already arrived and was stretching when she entered the room. The look on her face reminded me how overwhelmed I was the first time I went to the auditions. So I introduced myself, "Hi, I am Venna Bishop. Is this your first angel audition?"

"Yes, she replied, "I'm Laura Martinez, my friends call me La La. My husband and I saw your interview with Dr. Robert H. Schuller the Sunday when you flew in as an angel and landed on him. It was hilarious! Nick, my husband, thought I could be an angel too."

"Absolutely!" I replied, and immediately introduced her to some of the other angels while we continued stretching. Try-outs followed and while the panel of judges were deliberating, I said, "La La, copy the tentative rehearsal schedule." She looked rather bewildered as I handed her a copy of the rehearsal schedule and said again, "Copy the schedule."

La La, replied, "We don't know who made it yet." Then she began to wonder if my encouragement went with the positive thinking theme of the Crystal Cathedral.

I just smiled and said, "This is only a tentative copy of the rehearsal schedule. You will be glad you made a copy now rather than waiting. Sometimes they wait until the next day to call and tell us the results. You don't have access to the schedule then. This way you will have the schedule." La La finally obliged. The first time I arrived at rehearsal, I was happy to see La La had made the cut and our friendship evolved. La La continued her angelic flying for the next five years. (Eighteen years later La La is still actively participating in the general cast.)

The thirty-minute Angel Bible study before each angel rehearsal was a time of bonding with one another. During the years I performed, we studied various chapters of the book "Angels, Angels, Angels" by Billy Graham or we studied some of the Biblical characters connected with the pageants. Dorie or one of her assistant choreographers led the Angel Bible studies. (Gayle Carter Carlin, Jacquelyn Coffey, and Gary Iversen were her assistants when I was a flying angel.) The sharing and prayer times held during the Angel Bible studies were an expansion of the Cathedral's ministry. This fellowship time was a wonderful source of inspiration – a place where encouragement and support were available.

The angels are "grounded" during the first six weeks of rehearsals. Each move is choreographed to music. Everyone must learn the choreographed arm movements to all of the music and be able to perform it without thinking about it, before taking flight.

An angel's first flight is at technical rehearsal. We are provided with a harness, which looks much like a corset only thicker and heavier. The straps are made of leather and padded a half-inch thick, which supports our shoulder and legs. Attached to the leather are some metal hooks. The harness pinches when you're hanging from the wires. So Debbie Zubiate, who only weighed 90 pounds, stuffed some padding between her bones and the straps to serve as a cushion. I never had that problem, since my body had its own natural padding.

I imagine every angel that ever flew has vivid memories of her first flight. The first time I flew was on a Saturday night at 9:00 PM. There were three angels. Penny Salisbury, Trica Fletcher, and I were standing at the top of the West balcony in our leotards and tights without the gown parts of our costume. (We don't wear our complete costumes, until later in the rehearsal schedule.) The harness was strapped around my body and I was sure any extra body tissue was oozing out the sides.

The angel pilots were about to launch me when to everyone's surprise; Dr. Robert H. Schuller started climbing up the steps of West balcony. I couldn't imagine Dr. Schuller being out this late with an early service the next morning.

When Dr. Schuller got to the top of the balcony, he looked at me and said, "Venna Bishop! I heard about you, and I know your story. It is something."

My mind started wondering how I must look wearing nothing but leotards and tights, strapped in this tight harness with my extra parts oozing out, standing in front of a pastor.

Dr. Schuller went on to say, "So you are a Bishop, are you? I never heard of any Bishops who were angels."

We all laughed, and then I quickly challenged him saying, "Dr. Schuller we would like to invite you to fly."

A bit stunned by my invitation and before anyone could really take action, Dr. Schuller replied, "I have a sermon to preach in the morning, and I'd better be sharp for that. I really came to say thank you to everyone for volunteering your time to be a part of this glorious Christmas message." He concluded by having us join him in prayer for our safety and the joyful message we would bring to others. After the prayer, Dr. Schuller left with Bruce Hollenbeck, his faithful security escort.

After being hooked up to the wires, the initial five feet of lift above the balcony seats doesn't seem very high, until you're flying over the main floor. I imagine every angel who has flown forgets a part of their choreography on their first flight. That is why it is so essential to focus and learn it so well during ground rehearsal. Flying adds another dimension, when we soar nine stories above the audience and descend to three feet above their heads.

The first time Jill Holloway Delaney flew she was asked if she was scared. "No, Jill replied, "I have a lot of faith." At night, it doesn't seem as high because the lights are low. But on Children's Day in the daylight, things look different. Looking out of the 10,000 windows of the Cathedral, we realize we are above the tops of the trees. From the angel loft the hundreds of school buses and all the children in the parking lot also appear smaller in size.

Children's Day is a favorite performance for the angels. Often the children think the flying angels are real. After seeing the performance some children dream about being a flying angel. Jill Holloway Delaney wanted to be an angel from the time she was a little girl and saw her mother, Claudia Holloway, fly as an angel. Jill noticed the joy it brought her mother. It wasn't until Jill wore the wings herself that she realized the meaning of being an angel. Claudia flew for ten years, but the Children's Day she flew next to her daughter, Jill, will be the flight Claudia will always cherish the most. There have been other daughters since then who have followed their mothers in flight.

During one of the children's shows there was a power outage. According to Sandie Morgan, a seventeen-year veteran, the transformer on Garden Grove and Lewis Avenues quit, and the shows technical support was not available. The show continued with Shepherd Bradley Baker, singing "O Holy Night," without music or a microphone.

When it came time for the angels to fly, the angels walked down the steps from their angel lofts in the East and the West balconies. They stood on the balcony landing near the railing and did their choreography to "Angels We Have Heard On High." The children were so excited to see them up close, they didn't seem to mind a "grounded" angel flight.

After several years of performing in different types of angel costumes, Richard Bostard designed a simply magnificent angel gown and that concealed all the mechanics of flying. Dorie taught us choreography that flowed gracefully with the music enhancing the elegance of costume by allowing the pleated delicacy of the wings to move freely, giving the illusion of flight.

Each year the angels are taught a new variation. It is a beautiful sight when three angels from the East balcony and three from West balcony fly up and down in synchronization with one another and create a mirror image of their choreography. Sometimes, to the audience, the movements are so graceful, it appears as if the angels fly across the full length of the Crystal Cathedral.

There are 287 steps, with three sets of stairs, from the angel/dancers dressing room to the top of angel loft. Originally, with three shows a night, it involved four round trips between the dressing room and the angel loft. (2009 steps) There is a weight restriction for auditioning to be an angel, but that is easy to maintain during the shows with all those steps in between flights. (Some years we even had four shows a night on the weekends prior to Christmas and Easter.)

During the Glory of Easter, there are six angels. Three fly from the East balcony and three from the West balcony. The hosts of angels only fly once at Easter, for less than sixty seconds, but when we do fly we bring the good news of Christ's resurrection.

Marcia Worthington wanted to be a trapeze

artist when she was young. Flying as an angel gave her a feeling of being free from the daily stress of life. It was the closest she would ever come to swinging through the air from a trapeze. One evening, while flying over the West balcony with her arms extended, she leaned forward a little too far, lost her balance, and did a 360° flip! Within seconds, she had completed an unexpected angelic summer-sault above the audience, without a net. It took a few moments for her embarrassment to subside. Then her angel pilots made a quick adjustment to her harness before the next flight, so it wouldn't happen again.

Evidently, Marcia was destined for unusual flying endeavors. The angel loft is fairly dark during the pageants. The cloud machine in the loft begins operating, while the angel pilots attach the wires in the tracks to the hooks on an angel's harness. On one particular evening, Marcia flew out of the cloud from the angel loft as usual, only to find she was facing the audience in the West balcony. Somehow the wires got twisted, when they were attached to her harness. Instead of facing the main floor, she flew out backwards and was looking only at those people sitting in the West balcony. Naturally, the audience in the West balcony loved seeing her beaming face while she gracefully continued her choreography for their enjoyment.

In addition to her trapeze experiences, Marcia had some other special experiences during her five years of flying. A family of three daughters informed Marcia they had purchased 4 tickets for the performance. They were sad when they arrived, because one ticket was for their mother who had passed away. Seeing Marcia fly that night, helped them realize their mother was flying with the Lord and free from pain.

While waiting for cues in the angel loft, the angels would read, write letters, even knit by the light of miniature book lights. Trica Fletcher was studying sign language. It was fascinating to watch her practice signing to the songs being sung during the show.

Debbie Zubiate remembers the year they carried trumpet horns. The horns were about five feet long and heavy and got caught in the wires. That made it impossible to do the choreography gracefully.

In 1987 blond wigs for the angels were added to the costume. They were shoulder length and blond in color, rather bushy, kinky curly and quite a contrast to Mary Joy Dollente Bustos lovely Filipino features. The wigs were affectionately called Dolly Parton wigs, since they resembled some of Dolly's hair styles. Fortunately, the wigs were discarded shortly after the show opened.

Before the audience is allowed inside the Cathedral, the angels take their costumes to the angel lofts and hang them up, until time to put them on during the show. We avoid sitting in the costumes waiting for our cues, since the pleating is delicate and care is taken to keep them nice. We have cues for different positions at various times in the show. One year the cue to get dressed was during the singing of "Silent Night." Generally, "Silent Night" only has three verses. But this particular year, it had five verses with two of the verses repeated. There was an instrumental verse, and 4 vocals. Mary sang a verse alone, then Joseph sang, followed by a child soloist and then Mary and Joseph repeated a verse together. There was plenty of time during all those verses to get ready for a cue.

Angel safety is always a priority with the angel pilots. There have been a few times when an angel may have been stuck for a short time on an angel track, had their costume sweep the balcony rail, or encountered a bruise getting too close to a piece of the set, but over all those incidents have been very few and minor. Only once did an angel land on the main floor, but she returned to fly again.

To convey our thanks to our angel pilots for their commitment and dedication to our safety, the flying angels host potluck dinners each season between shows for the pilots and technical support staff. Homemade dishes of food always impressed them. One year we really pleased them, by giving the angel pilots sets of Air Force Pilot Wings! Sometimes the dancers joined us for our potlucks. Another year Dr. Schuller came, which really made a hit with the technicians.

For most of the angels, flying is a spiritual experience. Laura (La La) Martinez said, "It was a way to use the ballet lessons I took as a child to show honor to God, to represent Him in such a way, that I would touch so many people from around the world."

Gayle Carter Carlin was Dorie's first assistant choreographer, also a role model and leader of the Movement Choir. With her lovely red hair, she was a beautiful Angel Gabriel who flew for ten years. Gayle said, "Flying as an angel and serving in a leadership capacity is a way of sharing my faith not with words but by my actions. When you feel close to God in all that you do, you convey that connection to others, and it is portrayed to the audience."

Gayle was a project manager for a company known today as Raytheon/Hughes. Her boss was a confirmed atheist. He was proud of the fact that he had never stepped inside a church. Imagine Gayle's surprise when he asked for two tickets to the Glory of Christmas. He took his wife to the pageant and a short time later his wife passed away. Perhaps it was Gayle's involvement that opened the door and led them inside a church.

Heidi Inhelder Strickler was a flying angel, when she encouraged her sister Gina to audition to be an angel. Gina had been living in Atlanta and had returned to be with her family in California. Their parents had been involved in the Glory productions for many years. Patti, their Mom, played one of the wives for the Innkeeper and King Herod. Ken, their Dad, was a priest in the Sanhedrin court. Heidi's husband, Mark Strickler, is an angel pilot. Their family had established some close friendships within the Glory cast.

Gina admits, "My sister was always more interested in dance and ballet than I was." At first, Gina was hesitant to audition, since she was busy working as the Urban Outreach Instructor at the Crystal Cathedral and with the Youth Group. Heidi continued to encourage Gina to try-out. She even proceeded to show Gina some of the choreography that might help her during the auditions.

Gina finally agreed to go and said, "I really wasn't paying attention when I tried out, until my sister told me I got the part. I couldn't believe it!" She went on to say, "Then my sister and I got tickets for the preview night of Glory of

Christmas for my grandmother, parents, aunt, and uncle to sit in the South balcony. We knew we would be flying opposite each other. We would be flying directly in front of where they would be sitting in the South balcony." Gina continued, "I flew on angel track #3 from the East balcony and Heidi flew on angel track #4 out of the West balcony with her husband, Mark, as her angel pilot. What a thrill it was for us to fly right in front of my grandmother and the rest of our family. It will always be the most cherished and meaningful Glory of Christmas moment for our entire family."

Several months later Gina was in a serious automobile accident that resulted in a spinal cord injury. Cast members from Glory productions came to the hospital to pray and support her family. A steady stream of friends from the Cathedral came to see her. Carol Schuller Milner gave her communion on Good Friday. The nurses teased Gina, by saying they would set out a sign with her name on it pointing to "Gina's Room."

Gina is paraplegic and still in physical therapy. Instead of flying as an angel, she is flying high with self-confidence by showing and touching others with her efforts to be self-sufficient. She has her own apartment and a car. Currently, she is working on a master's degree program in theology at Biola University. Gina admits, "It is the heart of people at the Crystal Cathedral, the Jr. High Pastor Jeff Slack, my faith, and that of my families' that sustains me. I know God's angels are watching over me!"

Dorie Lee Matteson taught hundreds of angels to fly during her tenure as choreographer. After more than twenty years, she resigned her position as Assistant Director/Choreographer to focus on her teaching and writing careers.

Assuming this delightful task of choreographing angel flights is Tanya Durban. Tanya is really excited about the technical changes on the rigging they will be making for the 25th anniversary of the Glory of Christmas. She says, "These changes will give the angels more freedom of movement to turn around during their angelic flights." It provides a way to be more creative with the choreography and their lovely costumes will flow more freely. It will give the flying aspect of the angels a new and exciting dimension. Flying angels have always been an audience favorite. Imagine these heavenly hosts soaring even more freely, proclaiming the good news of God's love and salvation for all!

Psalm 91:11 "For He shall give His angels charge over you, To keep you in all your ways."
Possibilities Thinkers Bible The New King James Version

Praise Him with Dance

Dorie Lee Matteson was a senior at the University of Southern California working on a degree in dance, when 'God led her to the Crystal Cathedral' to do research for a school paper on dance and theology. Both the Old and the New Testament underline the importance of dance in the adoration and worship of God. For Dorie, dance is a heartfelt way to communicate with God and with others about God.

Dorie's interest in combining theology and dance was ideal for teaching ballet classes at the Crystal Cathedral. This also led to the formation of the Movement Choir, a musical interpretive dance group. The choir performed in conjunction with an Hour of Power interview guest, from the American Sign Language Institute, and also at some of the Sunday evening services. During this time Dorie began as the Choreographer for the Glory of Christmas followed by the Glory of Easter pageants. For ten years she was also a solo dancer and a flying angel. In addition to choreographing the pageants, she later became the Assistant Director for the pageants. At the same time, she completed her studies for a Master's degree in theology from the Fuller Theological Seminary. With more than twenty years as the Choreographer/Assistant Director, Dorie choose to pursue her passion to teach at the university level and finish writing her book focusing on her interests in combining theology and dance.

During her tenure as a choreographer, Dorie was a role model who inspired hundreds of dancers to share their faith as they performed. Many of the dancers had never been in a church. The Glory pageants were a wonderful way of ministering to them. She enjoyed watching how the Lord worked on young dancers, who had never met Him. Dorie remembered one dancer who heard Jesus tell Nicodemus while she was on stage, 'You have to become like little children in order to enter the Kingdom.' The dancer accepted Jesus that same evening.

Dancer auditions are held twice a year, usually September and February. Rehearsals begin immediately after auditions for dancers. The dancers are double cast with a couple of substitutes for back up. They are scheduled to perform on alternate nights. This allows some of the dancers to also participate in "The Nutcracker Ballet" during the Christmas season.

In the Glory of Christmas, the shepherd angel announces to the shepherds that a Savior is born in Bethlehem. Four more angels fly out to the music of "Gloria." Dancers are rejoicing on stage while they share in the joy of His birth with the flying angels. Identical twins, Cecilia and Teressa Dangeil, are among those dancers. Just as the music of Gloria comes to a crescendo, the twins, Cecilia and Teresa, lead the dancers performing "so ta chāy's" (split leaps) in unison down the ramp toward the south exit.

For several years, the twins danced together in the Glory pageants until Cecilia was cast for a part in "The Phantom of the Opera" in San Francisco for five years. Teresa remained in Southern California dancing in the Glory pageants. Since the angels and the dancers share a dressing room, it provided a chance to become better acquainted during the pageants. I had an opportunity to reconnect with Cecilia and watch her perform in "The Phantom of the Opera." She even invited me for an interesting back stage tour of the set.

Later that year I went to see the Glory of Christmas and watched Teresa dance again. While chatting after the performance, Teresa remarked about the difference in their roles. She smiled and teasingly said, "Cecilia is the rich twin doing the 'Phantom' and I am the poor twin dancing in the Glory pageants." Teresa went on to say, "I may not have the financial compensation, but I realize I am 'richer in spirit.' When I dance, it is to glorify the Lord."

Dancing on the Glory of Christmas set poses challenges for the dancers. Designed by Charles Lisanby, it is one of the largest sets in the world spanning 124 feet across. It becomes increasingly more difficult, when the main stage for the Glory of Christmas is on two levels with five steps in between. Maintaining balance and grace while dancing is essential anytime, but more so on different levels. The shepherds' hill consists of even more steps leading up to the first rail on the East balcony.

The Prelude for the Glory of Christmas features a pair of dancers beginning their dance at the top of the shepherds' hill. In 1989, Tanya Durban and Randy Masoner danced together in this opening scene to the music of "O Little Town of Bethlehem" performed by Roger Williams. Together they tell the Christmas story in dance while executing various dance steps going down the shepherds' hill and reaching out toward the Bethlehem Inn. Continuing the choreography they express, through their dance, the events that are about to unfold until they reach the manger. It is a beautiful piece of choreography, created by Dorie Lee Matteson, leading up to the betrothal scene of Mary and Joseph. Tanya didn't realize in 1989 when she danced this choreography, that fifteen years later, she would return as the choreographer for the Glory of Easter and Christmas–a position she currently holds.

After the birth of the Christ Child, there is a joyous scene with angels flying and dancers performing on stage to the music of "Angels We Have Heard On High." It is filled with glorious music and beautiful dance choreography. Tanya and Randy are among the group of dancers who are dancing the full length of the center ramp. Tanya's lovely long dark hair extends down the length of her back almost to her knees. At one point, Randy proceeds to do what is known in dancing terminology as a helicopter lift and Tanya's long hair wraps around his neck. As the music climaxes, they remain attached to one another held by Tanya's hair. It was hilarious to see Tanya dancing around in a circle attempting to unwind her hair from Randy's neck, while continuing down the center ramp toward the exit. Tanya chuckled and said, "I don't wear my hair that long anymore."

In the Glory of Easter, there are fewer dancers, since the pageant is a drama rather than a musical. The set is similar in size but involves many more steps and different levels. The dancers for the Easter productions are part of King Herod's Court, in a festive celebration during the Jewish Passover. Their costumes are quite elegant and they use many more scarves giving more drama to their dancing movements. In both pageants, the dancers have additional challenges to overcome. They must always be constantly aware of the "blessings" the animals leave behind that could affect one of their dance steps or landings. Tiptoeing in and amongst sheep droppings is something they do not have to cope with on most ballet stages.

Child soloists were added in 1992, when a wonderful dancer by the name of Ryan Turley came to auditions. His talent impressed the auditioning committee so much that they wanted to include him. So Dorie created the choreography and paired Ryan with another lovely child dancer, Lindsey Imler. Since then, child dance soloists have continued to be a part of the pageant. We would frequently see Dorie working with dancers of all ages after they performed. They would be in the hallways near the dancers' dressing room going over some steps to perfect their routines.

Special guest dance artists have been featured in different years. Kathy Thibodeaux and Richard K. Faucher were among the first guest dance soloists. In 1995 Heather Whitestone, the first physically challenged deaf Miss America in the pageant's history, danced in the Glory of Christmas. For Heather the various set levels posed an even greater challenge. Dorie experienced much joy in teaching Heather the choreography for the pageant. Heather was extremely focused, constantly counting her steps to memorize the routines. Dorie admitted that she was probably was the more tired than Heather after their rehearsals. It was Heather's determination and their combined positive faith, that made it a winning combination.

Joining one of the casts for the 25th anniversary will be professional dancers from the American National Ballet Company. Tanya is excited about the possibility of having various ballet companies featured each year. Tanya also choreographs for the Orange County Pacific Symphony Orchestra, the Performing Arts Center, and directs a ballet school in Costa Mesa.

Tanya's most rewarding times occurred last year on an opening night of the Glory of Christmas. Several of the girls and guys dancing came to her and said, "Tanya, we have never heard this story about Jesus before." While the show was going on, she saw several of dancers with tears on their faces.. Tanya noticed how touched they were. After the performance the dancers told her they were going to look into what this story is all about. Tanya said, "That was the most rewarding aspect to me, more than the artistic side of the production." Tanya continued, "I know that when it touches even one person that means more to me than anything. I am a perfectionist. I work the dancers hard during rehearsals. We train hard through the shows." Tanya admitted, "When it comes to what the show really is about, I keep reinforcing that spiritual aspect with the company. It puts every-thing into perspective for all of us. To look over and see your dancers with tears on their faces and desiring to learn more and not being closed off, that is my reward!"

Psalms 149:3 "Let them praise His name with dance."
Possibility Thinkers Bible - The New King James Version

THE GLORY OF TECHNICAL SUPPORT

Hooks, Cables & Shackles

In the very first production of the Glory of Christmas, an illusion of a flying angel was created by using a cardboard angel attached to a stick behind a backlit sheet. It was the actress, Mary Martin, who suggested to Dr. Robert H. Schulller that he consider adding live "flying angels." Most theatrical flying at that time was under the direction of Peter Foy and his company, "Flying by Foy." Some of Peter Foy's credits include the Broadway production of "Peter Pan" with Mary Martin and "Tinker Bell" at Disneyland

Because of Mary Martin's idea, Peter Foy was contracted to fly a live angel in the 1982 Glory of Christmas pageant. At that time, Edward Quiroga*, who had been a lead rock and roll singer for 15 years, knew that work was scarce so he accepted a technical support position at the Crystal Cathedral. Eddie helped install Peter Foy's first set of angel tracks. Dorie Lee Mattson, who was also the choreographer for the pageant, became the first live flying angel. Dorie recalls numerous adjustments being made to the tracks and the wire positions on her flying harness before she could fly. Eddie was intrigued with the technical aspects. It wasn't long before he established himself as the official in-house rigger.

Every year during technical week, Eddie as Technical Supervisor/Head Rigger, is responsible for the installation of 1200 feet of angel track prior to the Glory of Christmas. Timing is essential and the work must be done in less than a week to have the building available for regularly scheduled church services.

The tracks come in pieces 10 to 20 feet long and are assembled on-site into 70 to 80 foot lengths. They are then attached with cables and shackles at 5 foot increments, hoisted upward, and attached to the ceiling. The shortest track is 40 feet long, while others are set for 150 to 180 feet of travel. Keeping the tracks straight and level is critical during installation. This provides a smoother, quieter, and more effective angel flight. Some tracks are removed after Christmas and the rest are removed after the Glory of Easter and stored until fall.

Eddie and his team also work with lighting designer, Glenn Grant, to install the trusses that hold the lighting instruments. Chain motors are used to hoist the truss inside the Crystal Cathedral building, where the lights are assembled into the required configuration. The trusses are raised to a level so a team of workers can stand comfortably and install the par cans, lekos, spots and robotic instruments as determined by Glenn, the lighting designer. The trusses are then lifted and hung 60 feet above the floor.

Since the Crystal Cathedral is made of 10,000 glass windows, focusing of the lights must be done at night. There have been times when 450 lighting instruments were used compared to about half that amount in a Broadway show. Imagine spending all night in a rigging harness, hanging from the ceiling, focusing and locking down each of the lighting instruments, one light at a time.

During the preparation for the Glory of Easter, the Producer/Director, Paul David Dunn, and the Assistant Director, Terry Larson, and Production Stage Manager, Tom Larson walked into the Technical Shop with a video tape of an "Hour of Power" soloist David Meece singing "I can See." It had been suggested by Arvella Schuller that they might want to incorporate this music into the Glory of Easter in some way. These three directors were looking for suggestions as to how to use it and who might sing it. Immediately one his co-workers popped up and said, "Eddie can sing it." Surprised by their rigger's hidden singing talent, Eddie auditioned and was selected for the part of the Blind Man, in a scene that takes place on the temple steps during the Passover.

On the third day of the Jewish Passover, Jesus spent the day teaching on the temple steps. Many of the religious leaders were wondering where Jesus came from. Some were convinced he was sent from God because of the extraordinary teaching and the miracles he performed. Others felt he was a false prophet because he healed on the Sabbath—a day when no work was to be done. Concerned about Jesus' growing influence, the Sanhedrin met with the Roman centurion.

Later a heated discussion took place between the Sanhedrin and Jesus as to just who "sent" him. To substantiate his claim, Jesus took some mud from the pool of Siloam, placed the mud on the eyes of a man, blind from birth, and told him to wash his eyes in the waters of Siloam. (Siloam in Hebrew translated means "sent".)

Eddie, in the role of the Blind Man, after washing his eyes, rises from the pool and realizes his sight is fully restored. He starts singing the song "I Can See! . . . I can see who walks with me, I can see who knows my name." As he continues singing he walks over to spend a moment with his petite stage mother, Winnie

Herndon. She was weeping genuine tears, which glistened and streamed down her cheeks. It was one of those in-character moments for the two of them, which reflected the joy of the miracle that occurred as they conveyed it to the audience.

In recent years, Eddie has assumed the role of Judas. Eddie credits Bodie Newcomb* for sharing some insights with him about Judas, while Bodie was researching his own role as Jesus. Eddie was interested to learn that Judas was a man of means and educated. He came from money and was selected as the disciples' financial advisor, but Judas also had an "attitude."

On-stage, Eddie tries to illustrate those traits in Judas's character in the opening scenes, as he remains aloof from the rest of the disciples. He acts distant, as if he is above them, because of Judas' background. Eddie wants the audience to be wondering, "Which one is Judas?"

Eddie shared this comment, "What a contrast it has been going from the character of the Blind Man, adored and admired by audiences, then becoming Judas and feeling scorned and looked upon with such distaste. It's as if they would like to 'set you on fire'!"

In either role, Eddie does his best to become the character he is portraying, while at the same time keeping a watchful eye on all the technical aspects of his real full-time job. It is ironic that a "Blind Man" would also be tending to any rigging challenges that might occur during a show. To flying angels, it is comforting to know Eddie is always on the scene, insuring our safety and, along with Peter Foy's representative, Eugene Mendoza, guarding our angelic flight paths.

Angel Pilots

How does someone learn to "fly an angel"? Being an angel pilot involves learning to fly "stage bricks" before flying a live human being. "Stage bricks" are rectangle weights made of solid steel approximately 12" long by 2" thick and 5 inches wide. These bricks serve as counterweights in theater for raising and lowering changes of scenery. Flying these stage bricks is part of the angel pilot auditioning and training process.

It was Mary Martin who initially suggested "real" flying angels to Dr. Robert H. Schuller. "Flying by Foy" was commissioned to make flying angels a reality in the pageant. Peter Foy provides all the apparatus needed to make that possible. His Broadway production credits and company's reputation are well known within the entertainment industry. In addition to flying Mary Martin in "Peter Pan," Peter Foy has made concert tours with many stars such as Garth Brooks, Paula Abdul, EFX with Michael Crawford and Disney's "Beauty and the Beast."

A "Flying by Foy" representative is present at each show to inspect and insure the safety of the audience and everyone involved in the flying operation.

Eugene Mendoza, Foy's Flying Representative, flew angels before becoming a flying angel supervisor. He was also one of my dedicated angel pilots and a special friend to me personally. His 20 years of commitment and loyalty to the Glory pageants made him a prime candidate for training to be the on-site Foy Representative, a position Eugene has held for the past five years and continues to hold.

The angels and pilots are required to take positions in the angel loft before the house opens (theater talk for the time before the public is allowed inside the Crystal Cathedral.) The angel lofts are located above the East and West balconies of the building. They compare in size to small angular bedrooms without any heating. The angel lofts are even chillier and more uncomfortable when the Santa Ana winds are blowing.

In addition to the flying and cloud making equipment in the loft, there are 3 angels plus their costumes, 6 pilots, and a flight supervisor. With such tight quarters, we had many hours to get acquainted and share in-depth conversations while waiting for our cues. People brought mini flashlights to do homework, read, write Christmas or Easter cards or play games. We would often just watch the show, or share life's challenges and pray together. It was also an opportunity to witness to those who had never been in a church. Amazing things would occur in the angel lofts and even a romance might begin to flourish.

Mechanically, angels are flown using a winch and pulley system with cables attached to a track and a harness on the angel's body. It takes two angel pilots to fly one angel. One angel pilot hand cranks the angels as they go forward and backwards on the track. Compare this hand crank to operating a one-pedal bicycle. The second pilot moves the angel up and down electronically by pushing buttons. All angel pilots wear headsets. The production or stage manager cues the angel pilot on the radio. For example, one season I flew as an angel on track #3 and the assistant production manager, R. Derek Swire, called the cue "Stand by for Angel 3."

At that moment, my angel pilots directed me to stand on the tiny launching platform. They connected the two wires, which were attached to the cable in the track, to the hooks that were on the harness I was wearing under my costume. The Angel Supervisor would double-check the connections and in less than 90 seconds, the pilots would acknowledge, "Angel 3 standing by."

There were two other angels in the same loft

going through the same process with their pilots. At the "Go" call, our pilots would launch us out of a cloud over the audience as we did our ballet choreography to taped music by members of the London Philharmonic Orchestra. The synchronization for flying can range from nine stories high to just three feet above the heads of the audience, creating the illusion that we are floating above the audience. For me, each angel flight produced a rapturous feeling as I gazed into the eyes of the audience. I knew I was delivering a small part of God's message of forgiveness, hope, joy, and love.

The angel pilots have their fun, sometimes competitive, moments as they await the "Stand by for return" call followed by "Return-Go!" It is then they enjoy seeing who can crank their angel back into the clouds and angel loft the fastest, but still maintain some semblance of gracefulness for the audience. They like to claim we fly 40 mph, although I am not sure anyone has officially measured the speed.

Eugene Mendoza, Foy's Flying Representative, readily admits, "There is something about the Crystal Cathedral and the Glory pageants that keep you coming back. You know how the show is supposed to run. You've done it over a thousand times and sometimes, not every night cause we are all human, just sometimes when the house is packed, it's chilly, and it feels exactly like you are there! It just all comes together in a way that works just as God intended."

Eugene recalls a scene in the Glory of Christmas where nearly everyone in the cast is on stage. It is toward the end of the pageant and the 3 Wise Men, members of their entourage, singers and dancers are all kneeling before the Manger with Baby Jesus, Mary, and Joseph. The music of the first verse of "Hark, the Herald Angels Sing" is exuberant with flying angels descending from the east and west and returning to their angel lofts. As the music dissolves from a crescendo to a diminuendo, the cast of 100 freezes in position and a reverent stillness descends over the audience.

During this interlude, Eugene flies the solo angel #7. She gracefully ascends above the starlit sky of Bethlehem and you hear the words to the second verse, *Christ by highest Heaven adored.* As the words continue, *Christ the everlasting Lord,* Eugene is profoundly aware of the moment, sensing the audience's anticipation. "It is a scene reflecting exactly how the first Christmas was," he replies, "Cold, brisk, winter air, very still as a glorious angel flies toward the manger to the music, *Late in time behold him come, off-spring of the favored one.*

Eugene continues, "The quietness of the

scene touches us in a way, that it appears to be exactly as if we are there—each individual, an angel and the Baby Jesus. Still, you realize there are almost 3000 people in the audience, 100 cast members on stage, animals, camels, various colors and different lighting effects. Yet, everyone is focusing on this glorious scene and that is what makes it all worthwhile. It touches us, and we cling to the moment when it must have happened exactly as we are experiencing the wonder."

From Herding Sheep to Lighting Design

From Volunteering to Paid Employment

Glenn Grant started as a teenage volunteer shepherd, herding sheep in the second Glory of Christmas. Since then, he has been involved in the Glory of Christmas and the Glory of Easter pageants by filling in as a substitute or being assigned to almost every major male role at one time or another. He never dreamed his volunteering endeavors would spark his career interests and lead him to his current position as lighting designer for all the events held at the Crystal Cathedral.

Glenn's first paid position in the pageant was working animal clean-up known more affectionately as a "pooper scooper." There were amusing moments. The 60 mph Santa Ana Winds were nearly unbearable during one of the Glory of Easter shows. Glenn had his rolling mop bucket and proceeded outside through the East door of the building. Somehow the wind got hold of the mop bucket. It went rolling and bumping along the sidewalk, jumping the curb all by itself, landing back on its wheels and traveling directly out into the South parking lot. The wind was taking the speeding mop bucket right toward the front of a car. Glenn went racing out after it, then suddenly noticed the driver's glassy eyes transfixed on the mop bucket. The driver appeared to be frozen in the front seat of his car . . . he did not budge! Luckily, Glenn outran the wind and caught the flying mop bucket just in time. Glenn has a vivid memory of the driver's perplexed and bewildered look as he focused on the mop bucket racing toward him.

After catching "flying mop buckets," Glenn auditioned to catch "flying angels" as an angel pilot. He was my angel pilot at one of the Glory of Christmas pageants. He seemed to take piloting me, as the most mature angel, in his stride. Although flying younger angels may have appealed more to him as a young man, he always made me feel graceful. I was just like one of them.

The following Glory of Easter Glenn started operating a follow spot, which resembles a giant sized flashlight on stilts. Operating a follow spot requires steadiness and concentration, not an easy task when the main character suddenly changes direction to side step unexpected animal droppings. Glenn continued perfecting his skill at running follow spots at his school plays in Pasadena. His volunteer endeavors in this area sparked his interest to pursue a degree in Film and TV Production.

Through the years, Glenn's dedication provided him an opportunity to assume responsibility for several different stage manger positions. One of his early challenges, as a young teen stage manager, was managing the Tustin High School Football players who were cast that year as Roman Soldiers in the Glory of Christmas. Their participation was a community service project and their team received a donation for their support. Still vivid in Glenn's mind was the evening three of the more hefty football players were ready to do battle against one another in the parking lot. Imagine stepping forward, weighing a mere 150 pounds, and attempting to diffuse their argument. It was going to be a real test of his managerial abilities as he chose to use the power of words instead of muscle to settle the situation.

Glenn credits Tom Larson, his Production Stage Manager, for teaching him some tremendous people skills in working with volunteers. For Glenn the message was clear. When working with a cast of volunteers, he would ask, "Why are you here? What is your purpose for volunteering?"

On another occasion Glenn had to separate

two squabbling adults at the beginning of a scene on the Shepherds' Hills of Bethlehem. He gently asked, "Is this the Christmas message the Lord wants you to convey to the cast and audience? Isn't your goal to work as a team and share this glorious story with others?"

Glenn's approach clearly had an impact on one of these ladies as she brought home baked cookies to Glenn at the very next performance, with more cookies for each of the following shows in which she was scheduled. What a compliment to Glenn and certainly an appropriate way to apologize to a growing young stage manager.

Singing is not one of Glenn's talents. Imagine his dilemma when he was asked to substitute for Joseph, who sang two songs with Mary in the Glory of Christmas. (The real Joseph had laryngitis.) The first song comes after the Angel Gabriel appears to Mary telling her she is with child. Mary starts singing the "Magnificat." Joseph joins her and they finish the song together. After Baby Jesus is born they join one another singing a verse of "Silent Night."

Fortunately for Glenn, the music was on tape and he could lip sync the words. He was feeling quite confident of his singing abilities after lip syncing the first part of the song, until . . . he suddenly realized the words he had memorized were not the same as the ones being sung on tape to the audience. Panic set in as he turned his head away from Mary and faced up stage. Realizing his predicament, he just gazed at the stars above the set keeping his head held high until the music ended. He made doubly sure the second time he was asked to fill in for Joseph that he received the right words.

Instead of having to spend every night at the pageants as a stage manager, Glenn chose to usher for a couple years when he was in college majoring in Film and TV Production. He found it intriguing that people came from around world with one specific purpose in mind—to attend the Glory of Christmas or the Glory of Easter. "It was amazing," Glenn exclaimed, "usually they visit California to go to Disneyland!"

Volunteering and seasonal positions had filled Glenn's leisure hours, but it was time to get serious about seeking a real job. About that time Perry Halford, one of the lighting designers, resigned. It was the beginning of Glenn's official role as a lighting designer and an opportunity to implement his computer-aided design skills.

For each pageant or event at the Crystal Cathedral, Glenn designs all the plots (plans or maps showing the physical location of each light fixture) and the different scene levels and positions on the computer. He determines where lighting instruments are hung at various points on the trusses and in other areas throughout the building. He has 600 instruments at his disposal and uses a combination of color gels (translucent colored plastic) in the pageants.

The Glory of Christmas set has a dark background, in contrast to the Easter set, which looks white. Deep reds and rich colors against a dark set require special artistry and blending. The Easter set has its challenges, because it looks white to the naked eye. However, it has underlying green tones, which requires a different mixture of hues to keep it looking white. The robotic lights, also called intelligent lights, have some really unusual or dramatic features, which allow for more creativity. The downside is there is more opportunity to be a perfectionist, so it takes longer to program because of the variety of settings and the 16,000 color combinations available.

The board operator, Kris Silver, runs the lights during rehearsal, which gives Glenn an opportunity to make any design changes. After rehearsal is over the light crews continue working re-focusing some of the instruments. Frequently they are still on-the-job at sunrise. (Daytime focusing is not an option in a building constructed entirely of glass.)

Glenn's greatest joy and his biggest challenge is the lighting design for the "Hour of Power's" Christmas Eve program. Not only does the lighting for all seven Candlelight services have to be breathtaking for those attending, it also must be spectacular for the satellite television audiences worldwide. Also, the Glory of Christmas has two performances on December 23rd and begins again on December 26th. It requires making minimal changes to the pageant's settings, plus bringing in the necessary additional fixtures to adequately light for television, without destroying the ambiance needed for those attending the candlelight services. Is it any wonder that Glenn arrives at 3:00 p.m. on December 23rd and doesn't leave until the following evening on December 24th at about 10:00 p.m.?

For Glenn, the most satisfying aspect of his lighting design work is being a part of a creative team that is also able to provide a live Christmas Eve Candlelight Service broadcast around the world. It is a time of pressure but it is also his way of saying thanks to the men and women serving this great nation, who cannot be with their immediate families on Christmas. Glenn says, "It is definitely the single most gratifying night." He adds, "My small part is only a drop in the bucket, if that broadcast brightens some ones Christmas in the smallest way, makes them happy, and causes them to smile. It is my Merry Christmas present to the world!"

Extraordinaire Editing

To edit is to identify the essential elements needed to convey the message. The process may involve correcting, modifying, removing, replacing, revising, rearranging, or even deleting some of the content. This delicate task, for editing the short segments and videos of Glory of Christmas and Glory of Easter, is undertaken by Nancy Warshaw and Patrick Couchois, although their primary focus is editing the "Hour of Power" televised services each Sunday.

The Glory of Christmas and the Glory of Easter clips are aired in either 30 second or one-minute segments on the "Hour of Power." In the television industry, they are referred to as commercials.

Information conveyed in this short time frame includes the Big 5 W's —Who, What, When, Where, and Why. The executive director writes the copy or script and the off-screen narrator reads the information. This process is known as a voice-over. It is the editing department's responsibility to take the copy of the voice-over soundtrack . . . "The Glory of

Christmas at the Crystal Cathedral in Garden Grove, California will begin November 25th to Dec 30th. For tickets and information contact 714/54-Glory," and combine it with pictures.

Consider this — a one-minute commercial may take two days to prepare. The tricky part is selecting top quality pictures and the appropriate number of them to complement the voice-over within the allotted time. An added challenge for Nancy and Pat is that they must eliminate any photos which include actors who are members of the Actor's Equity Association. (Union employees under contract who receive a royalty for any promotional appearances.) This requires some ingenuity and creativity on Nancy's and Pat's parts, since some of the key roles involve "equity actors." For a Glory of Christmas commercial, it requires a more creative approach if either Mary or Joseph are a members of the Actor's Equity Association. Fortunately, the Baby Jesus is a toy baby doll and not an "equity" member.

Occasionally cast members in costume, along with some of the animals, will appear during an "Hour of Power" service to promote one of the Glory pageants. These are ideal times to obtain footage for future commercials, because the filming during daylight hours is more desirable. A jenny (also known as a female donkey) gave birth to a young foal (baby donkey.)

The Glory production staff, (Sandy Boselo and Cathy Dixon) decided it would be a great promotional idea to have the trainer/handler bring in the miniature mother donkey and her young foal during a service. The trainer led the mother donkey in on a leash. Another leash was used to connect the young foal directly to her mother. The donkey's arrival spurred a few "ooh's" and "aha's" from the congregation.

At the close of the interview, the trainer/handler turned to lead the mother toward the exit. Apparently, the young foal enjoyed the attention of the congregation. As the mother started down the center ramp, the young foal plopped down on his hind legs, dug in, and refused to move.

The mother was just as stubborn and began tugging and pulling her young foal, still seated on the ramp, despite her baby's resistance. The congregation erupted in laughter realizing at that moment the donkeys were upstaging Pastors Robert H. Schuller and Robert A. Schuller.

Cameramen were busy filming the entire scene. However, once Nancy and Pat reviewed the footage, they realized it could not be aired on television. The position of the donkey and the trainer's leashes made it appear on screen as though the trainer was pulling the young donkey, when in fact, it was the mother donkey that was really pulling the baby donkey.

Editing requires knowledge, creativity, ingenuity, and superb judgment—skills Nancy and Pat exercise with each broadcast, video, or commercial they produce.

As the author of this book, I also have a profound respect and admiration for the editing talents of Emily De Shazo. Her insightful direction and patience have guided me to improve my writing. I marvel at how Emily's skillful copyediting and ability to clarify a thought can make a reader's experience more enjoyable. I credit her editing skills with helping me to make this book a reality. The talents of individuals who do perform the editing tasks are essential to the success of the project, whether it is a television program, a video production, a script or a book.

THE GLORY of
PERFORMING

The Volunteers' Crown

The hundreds of volunteers in the general cast are the lifeblood that flows through the pageant and keeps the show alive and in motion. Their presence brings life to their scenes. Their teamwork makes it happen. Their spirit impacts the audience. Their humor keeps it flowing. Their energy is endless. Their commitment impresses staff. Their compassion for one another is loving. Their friendships are long lasting. All these qualities comprise the most valued and important participants in the pageants—the volunteers!

Why I Volunteer
It's not for money, not for fame.
It's not for any personal gain.
It's just for love of fellow man,
It's just to lend a helping hand.

It's just to give a tithe of self,
That's something you can't buy with wealth.
It's not for medals won with pride,
It's just for the feeling deep inside.

It's that reward deep in your heart,
It's feeling you have been a part.
Of helping others far and near.
That makes you a volunteer!
Annonymous

The general cast participates in the beginning (opening) scenes of the pageants. They are the foundation for the first major scenes in the pageants. In the Glory of Christmas, the general cast rejoices in the opening scene at the betrothal of Mary and Joseph and celebrates the announcement of their engagement. In the Glory of Easter the general cast welcomes Jesus of Nazareth into the city of Jerusalem singing and shouting, "Hosanna!"

The general cast flows through to the closing or final scenes of the pageants. In the Glory of Christmas, they are part of the Wiseman's entourage as they present their gifts, celebrate the birth of Jesus, and worship the newborn King. In the Glory of Easter, they open the show and many are not involved again until near the Crucifixion, which climaxes with the glorious resurrection of Jesus, the greatest "Amen" to God's handiwork.

Cast members sign up to participate when they read the announcement in the church bulletin. Rose Brown and her daughter, Christine, were walking out of the Cathedral one Sunday when Christine said, "Mom, you just indicated you wanted to do something different now that you are retired. Why don't you sign up to be a volunteer for the Glory of Christmas?

Rose responded, "I don't sing or dance. I'm not an actress."

Christine replied, "That doesn't mean anything. Go ahead, sign up.

Rose listened to her daughter's advice and signed up for the 2004 Glory of Christmas. Rose became one of the journey people traveling from Nazareth to Bethlehem to be taxed. She also carried the big red feather fan during the entourage of the Three Wise men. She didn't have to sing or dance or even act, but her presence along with other cast members was needed to make each of these scenes real and meaningful for the audience

Rose made many friends within the cast and among the ushers. After some costumes changes and climbing up and down the concourse stairs, she told her usher friend Fred, "Either make these stairs shorter or get me an elevator!"

Rose's greatest joy comes after the show, when she greets the audience in her entourage costume. A fourteen-year-old girl from Nigeria insisted on having her mother take her photo standing next to Rose. The girl was genuinely impressed with Rose's elegant costume. Another guest said, "I have lived in Orange County all my life and this is the first time I have seen this pageant. It is just remarkable."

Almost every cast member has heard similar comments or had their photos taken with guests after performances. Their photos will be on display in family scrapbooks of visitors who have attended the pageants from around the world. The comments the cast hears from guests after the pageants are their reward for the many hours they give of their time. Rose admits, "Being a part of the cast and performing was the best experience of my life."

Irene Zubiate has been in the pageants for twenty-three years. She has autographed pro-grams and had photos taken by people from Germany, Russia, and Holland, to name only a few. There have even been times when guests wanted her to pray with them after being touched by what they saw in the pageant. Par-ticipating in the pageant as a cast member or an usher is Irene's way of ministering to people who do not know Jesus.

Irene played the part of the first innkeeper's wife. When the innkeeper told Mary and Joseph the was no room for them in the inn, Irene, in the role of the innkeeper's wife said, "Isn't there something we can do?" Her impromptu line became a permanent addition to the pageant. Bodie Newcomb*, the current production stage manager, was in the role of the innkeeper at the time and told her to keep saying that line.

During the second Glory of Easter, the story of Jesus and His disciples visiting Mary and Martha was a part of the pageant. From that one performance Irene still remembers playing the role of Martha. For several years, Irene was a stage manager but she finds ushering less demanding during this period of her life.

Finch Booker felt blessed to be one of Jesus disciples in the Glory of Easter. He was cast in the role of the disciple, James the Less, and always made sure he had a beard in time for the pageant. One of the most meaningful moments for Finch was carrying his Lord and Savior from the cross over to the tomb for His burial. He felt the burden and the loss of his Master but with the resurrection came the joy of redemption.

Bruce Hollenbeck volunteered in the second Glory of Christmas. There weren't enough volunteers the first two years so they doubled up on parts. Bruce said, "I made 7 different costume changes in just one show and we had three shows a night." Originally, the opening scene began with everyone in pageboy outfits forming a huge cross on stage holding plastic candles. That scene was eliminated the following year.

The crucifixion scene during Easter was an emotional scene for the cast and especially for Bruce playing the part of a Roman soldier. Once again they doubled up on parts and the stage was darkened while Bruce, as a Roman soldier, helped nail Jesus to the cross.

Bruce said, "It wasn't easy to do and it took a tremendous emotional toll. Even gambling for Jesus' robe was a gut-wrenching experience when he looked up toward Jesus hanging on the cross." Still he had to stay in character playing the part of a Roman soldier and give the impression he did not care.

For a few years during the Glory of Easter, Vitalis and two Roman soldiers rode in from the East balcony on horses. Bruce, playing the part of a Roman soldier, walked in front of Jesus. Two more guards followed him carrying whips for the flogging scene, which would take place once they got into position. Walking past the audience seated on the East side, Bruce noticed two rows of Catholic nuns dressed in their traditional long black and white habits. Bruce said, "Memories of my Catholic school days immediately resurfaced, and the skin on the back of my neck began to crawl. I felt about four feet tall in my Roman soldier costume knowing they were glaring at me as if I was the enemy."

One of Bruce's most interesting performances as a Roman solider was when Jesus was brought before Pontius Pilate. The crowd below Pilate's balcony was yelling for Pilate to crucify Jesus. It was customary to release a prisoner each year during the Feast of the Passover. Pilate offered the crowd an option. He would release Jesus or the murderer Barrabas, but the person playing Barrabas was nowhere in sight.

Bruce said, "I immediately signaled Pilate with a theater signal to 'stretch and ad lib.' Then I took off my Roman soldier costume. Underneath was this white gown. Another member of the cast grabbed some dust and put it on my face and messed up my hair. Ninety seconds later, I was transformed into Barrabas." Just as the theater saying goes, 'The show must go on' and Bruce felt good about stepping into the part.

At one time, a series of fireworks was attached to the 90 foot Cathedral door. The fireworks were strung in a series that went from the bottom of the open door to the top. They were set to go off at the death of Jesus to symbolize the tearing of the curtain in the temple in Jerusalem. They began with a flash bang effect, but inside the Cathedral the noise was so loud and unexpected that one third of the audience were up on their feet before the fireworks stopped. Special effects by Rick Helgason are still a part of the show, but an earthquake has replaced the fireworks.

People of all religious backgrounds come to see the pageants from various locations around the world. One evening the ushers greeted a Muslim who was very excited to have finally arrived at the Crystal Cathedral. He asked, "Is this where the Jesus show is held?" After seeing the performance, he shared with Solon Goodson and other cast members that he had walked all day from Los Angeles to Garden Grove just to see the pageant. Everyone could see that he was thrilled to have seen the pageant and clearly felt that his long walk was more than worth the effort.

Picture three generations from one family participating in the pageants all at the same time! The Peterson Family attends the Catholic Church and has participated in the Glory productions for fifteen years. For the Peterson Family it is a family affair.

It all started when Suzanne Peterson's sister and her family, came to watch one of her sister's friends perform. Suzanne has been a Roman soldier, spot light operator and is currently supervising the angel pilots. Having been an angel pilot for ten years Suzanne said, "My goal is to be sure everything goes off smoothly every night and that everyone is safe during their flight."

Michael and Xavier are Suzanne's children. They participate in various children's scenes, mingling with the shepherds or circling the dancers. Michael and Xavier know just where they should be on stage, especially when it comes to helping a new cast member lead in a sheep or goat. Like many children in the cast, they enjoy carrying in the newborn lambs and kid goats.

Pat Peterson, Suzanne's mother, attends every show and has a key role in providing medical support. Her nursing skills are a necessity. She is present at every show to provide medical support along with other members of the medical team. Pat has also worked with security. During the Glory of Easter, she is one of the "cape women" assisting during the time Jesus and the two thieves are nailed to the cross.

Another volunteer Laura (La La) Martinez has experienced a unique perspective by participating in the pageants for eighteen years. She spent five years flying above the audience as an angel before joining the general cast on stage and looking directly at the audience.

La La has performed in the cast in a variety of roles from grinding grain or serving as a wine lady, to being one of the Kings' wives in Herod's scene or assisting a Wiseman with his robe in the entourage. She is responsible for various props, making sure they are returned to a certain place for the next scene. Her experience also helps with the training of new volunteers when they first join the cast.

Katherine (Kitty) Paladin and Claudia Holloway each played the role of Mother Mary in the first few productions of the Glory of Easter. During those years Mary was a general cast member. Claudia and Kitty each felt the emotional impact of what they learned about themselves in the role of Mary. When Jesus was nailed to the cross, the lights were darkened and the focus of attention was on Mary, the Mother of Jesus. The pain and loss when she cried was as piercing to each of them in the role of Mary, as it was to the audience.

Kitty said, "I look back on it with great reflection for what I learned. We were literally walking through the Bible. The script is so well done that it comes alive. That is the miracle, years later, it still comes alive!"

Kitty continued, "I remember going outside after the pageant to talk to people from the audience. They were so touched by the story of the Glory of Easter, that they couldn't even speak."

Kitty was excited to be on the ground floor as the very first Mother Mary in the Glory of

Easter. Blocking (staging) had to be done and there were so many people in the cast that the logistics were complicated. The producer and director did an amazing job of pulling it together. Kitty said, "I appreciate what had to be done then to make the pageants what they are today.

The youngest volunteer is Landon Christopher Mendoza. Landon is making an early debut as the Baby Jesus on the 25th Anniversary Brochure of the Glory of Christmas. Landon is the infant son of Eugene and Jennifer Mendoza. Eugene is Peter Foy's Flying Representative and has been with the cast twenty years. Eugene's first part in the pageants was as one of the village children and now, his son, is shown as Baby Jesus in the brochure. Other cast members are shown as Mary and Joseph. Kristy Cavinder who is a dancer and flies as an angel, is photographed as Mary, and Philip Ward who often plays a Roman soldier, is shown as Joseph.

Frequently the general cast volunteers must come directly from their daytime jobs to be at the Cathedral in time for show call. (Report time for cast members.) Details from checking out costumes, pre-setting the costumes, applying make-up or picking up props must be in place before the doors are opened to the general public. Dancers and angels stretch their muscles in the hallways and the concourse level buzzes with activity. There isn't time to stop to eat so a meal is provided when there are two or more shows in an evening. During some years, these meals were prepared and served by volunteers, but catering is easier and more efficient. Mealtime is short for people in the first scenes, and a hot meal at that time of night is really appreciated. It also becomes a time of bonding with other cast members.

David Lewis performed in the Glory Pageants in the early 1990's, before becoming the only white person in an all black entertainment group which toured throughout California. Things were going well, until the terrorist attack on New York City's World Trade Center and its aftermath.

There were also some family issues such as when his parents divorced. David moved back home to help his mother. The sadness became even more unbearable when his older brother passed away. His dad continued being a workaholic. Coping in her own way, his mom became a "foodaholic." David joined her in that "foodaholic" frenzy, overwhelming the scales at 501 pounds. Then they both realized that eating was a way of coping with their unhappiness and something had to change. Together they worked through the reasons for their addiction to food, and what they had to do about it.

While losing the weight, David asked himself one question, "What in my past has made me happy?"

He suddenly realized, "I am the happiest when I am working, especially when I am performing." Then he recalled the contentment he felt in the early 1990's, when he was volunteering in the Glory Pageants. A short time later he heard an advertisement on the radio announcing ticket sales for the Glory of Christmas. David called the Glory Production Office and asked, "Do you need any more volunteers?"

Bodie Newcomb*, the production stage manager, remembered David from his volunteer commitment to the pageants ten years ago. Bodie immediately assigned David a stage manager position and had him fill in on some of the group scenes.

David believes, "Working is being busy; it is not about money. It is about being active, involved, and fulfilled by being a part of something bigger than yourself."

The pageants offer him that opportunity. David continues to assume various roles. He is the Disciple Andrew in the Glory of Easter DVD. He was also a wardrobe assistant in the Once Upon All Time Creation production at the Crystal Cathedral.

What joy it is for David to reconnect with the hundreds of positive wonderful people he had worked with before. What amazed him were the children, who were now in their twenties, still volunteering or serving as stage managers.

David delights in encouraging his acquaintances to participate even if they have never been on stage before. Some have gone on to pursue a theatrical career because of their Glory experience.

David admits, "Participating in a pageant of this magnitude, recognized nationally, is an honor. I love having it on my resume!"

Julie Hara has been in the Glory pageants for seventeen years. Faithful and versatile, she has performed at least ten different roles. For six years, her daughter, Rita, spread her own wings as an angel, while proud mother, Julie, returned a smile from the stage below.

Another family, the Pereboom's eagerly await the pageants each year. Their entire family wishes the pageants would never have a closing night and are always delighted when a new season begins.

Penny attended services with her parents in 1974, when the Cathedral was known as Garden Grove Community Church. Later, at a Lutheran Church in Huntington Beach she met and married her husband, Wayne. Wayne

Pereboom sings in the church choir and directs the hand bell choir at their Lutheran Church.

Penny is a professional ice skater and teaches ice-skating. Her dream is to turn in her skate blades for flying angel wings someday. Until then, she is happy to be one of Herod's wives or in the Wise Men's entourage. Her daughter, Lisa, joins Penny in some of the group scenes. (Lisa is currently pursuing an elementary education degree at Concordia University.)

In the Glory of Easter, Jesus, played by Peter Uribe,* enters the temple in Jerusalem. The moneychangers are doing business in the courtyard of the temple selling sheep, goats, and doves. Wayne Pereboom, in the role of the pig man, is designated to carry a whip and bring in a squealing pig. At one performance, Wayne was absent so his son, Brian, a high school freshman, assumed the pig man's part.

The moneychangers in the temple and the squealing pig that Brian was carrying angered Jesus, played by Peter Uribe.* Peter, as Jesus, grabs the whip from Brian's hand and uses it to drive out the moneychangers. Evidently, Brian was standing a little too close to Jesus because the thrust from swinging the whip briefly stung Brian's hand. It got Brian's attention and reminded him of the importance of listening to the details when assuming another role.

Brian understands the need for accuracy. He plays a dozen different brass and woodwind instruments in band. His goal is to be one of the herald trumpeters in the pageants.

Collectively, the Pereboom Family has assumed over a dozen different roles in the cast and substituted often when needed. They value the fellowship with the volunteers, and are deeply moved to be able to tell this glorious story to others in this manner.

Some of the fathers are cast to be magi at Christmas and disciples at Easter. Sometimes Doug Carraway, Don Eldridge, Winston Covington and Brian Gould play these dual roles. Cynthia and Jessica Carraway join Doug in the general cast, while Debbie Eldridge is part of Don's entourage. Kaylee and Jeff Gould were most sympathetic the first time their dad tried to ride a camel. The camel had a difficult time getting up and Brian fell backwards receiving a swift kick to his head resulting in a black eye.

Richard (Rick) Brown has two opposing character roles, which demand different behaviors. He is the criminal Barrabas and also a disciple in the same performance.

Gary Larson, who plays the Disciple Thaddeus said, "The most difficult and most meaningful scenes are the crucifixion and burial of Jesus. Being on stage for those makes it real."

Eric Hornbell and his twin brother, Scott, were disciples when Bodie Newcomb* played Jesus. The scene begins with the twelve disciples arriving in the Upper Room for the Lord's Supper. The table, used for the Lord's Supper, is on a hydraulic lift and comes up from the stage floor prior to their arrival. It is dark on stage when the disciples enter the Upper room. They proceed by reaching for the stools stored under the table and sit down. One evening the click lock that held the table in place slipped. The disciples literally had to hold up the sinking table on their laps until the scene ended.

Cast members often try to inject humor with one another prior to or during a performance. The twins were no exception in their roles as disciples. They tried to outdo each other. Eric played the part of the Disciple Peter at the Lord's Supper. The time came for Bodie Newcomb,* in the role of Jesus, to wash Peter's feet. Kneeling down Bodie noticed that Eric, in the role of Peter, had painted a 'happy face' on one of his toes. Bodie, being a focused professional actor, didn't even hesitate and went on with his lines.

Linda (Schulz) Lane was in college the first time she performed in the pageants. She said, "It provided one more opportunity for our family to participate in an activity together. My sister,

Barbara, was a flying angel and I was a featured dancer."

Linda recalls dancing and twirling six-foot scarves in front of the camels. Sometimes the camels would spit on the dancers. Could it have been a camel's way of applauding their performance?

More than fifteen years later, Linda's teenage sons, Robby and Daniel, found some old photos of her dancing in the pageants. They were shocked but also fascinated with their mother's involvement. Linda home schools her sons. They agreed volunteering in the pageants would be an ideal drama class.

Linda, Robby, and Daniel Lane have performed in many different roles. They range from being scribes and messengers in Herod's and Pilate's Courts to being Roman soldiers in the marketplace or members of the Wise Men's entourages.

Robby and Daniel liked being Roman Soldiers. They begged their mom to become one, even though it was a male role. She finally agreed and admits it was an awesome experience. It became more meaningful during the filming of the newest Glory of Easter DVD. Linda is a Roman Soldier standing on stage between her two sons, one a sentry, the other a scribe. The DVD captures that special scene and is something she will treasure and share with her sons and – maybe even grandchildren.

Linda also recalls the bonding she experienced with her sons, while waiting their cues, and the jokes they shared before going on stage. Yet, nothing compares to their contact with the audience members after the performances. One of the guests asked, "Is it true? It is really true?"

Her oldest son replied, "Yes, it really is the real thing. Honest, it's true."

The guest was touched but so was Linda by her son's response. She knew the pageant experiences were helping to shape and form the values of her two sons.

"The message they exchanged is something that cannot be manufactured," Linda said, "It can only be treasured."

Pat Smith feels her involvement in the pageants is a blessing. Greeting the audience after the show is one of her joys. The experience was enhanced at times when she would join me outside the bookstore prior to and between shows. As the author of this book, I encouraged her to sign her name too, when anyone bought "Glory Stories" and wanted an autograph. Her reaction, along with other cast members who joined me from time to time, was one of delight. The individuals I wrote about in this book are the stars! I was merely the joyful storyteller.

Through the years, thousands of volunteers were filled with joy by participating in the pageants. They did not earn Oscar nominations for their performances but their dedication clearly merits recognition.

Revelation: 2:10 "Be thou faithful until death and I will give you a crown of life."

An Actors' Spiritual Connection

Each season actors affiliated with the Actors' Equity Association audition to be part of the pageants. For eighteen years, Alan Coates* has been invited to play the role of Pilate in the Glory of Easter. It is a role he delivers with conviction and authority.

Alan admits, "It is unusual for professional actors to commit to a production on a yearly basis. It is a spiritual connection; a need to be a part of the Passion Story that has deeply affected us all. We want to tell this great story and send the audience away having had a moving and meaningful experience"

Alan continued, "Each year a happy group of professional actors are proud to audition and return. We are growing and evolving as a 'company of actors' and delight in renewing friendships with the staff and volunteer cast members. It is like being a part of a family who trusts and relies on one another. It is an ensemble, and everyone who puts on a costume is a part of that ensemble."

"I get to work with committed professionals and an admirable cast of volunteers," Alan exclaimed. "It is not about me, but what live theater brings and offers us as an ensemble."

He admits, "I have great respect and admiration for any production that can survive in the Los Angeles/Hollywood area."

Originally from Cape Town, South Africa, Alan went to boarding and drama school in the United Kingdom before joining the Royal Shakespeare Company. The Company later performed on Broadway in New York. Alan was fascinated with the Broadway Theater. He fell in love with an American girl, became a citizen, and still lives in New York. He chuckles regarding the parallels of his British heritage. It was often British actors who were selected to play Roman characters in Biblical movies, and it is his British training that he brings to the role of Pilate.

Alan is especially grateful for the compassion shown by the cast and staff when his father passed away. Prior to the start of the Glory of Easter rehearsals, Alan spent four weeks at his father's bedside in Cape Town. His dad insisted what his son was doing was important and felt he should leave to participate in the Glory production.

Knowing they may never see each other again, Alan left with a heavy heart. It was an agonizing 27-hour flight to Los Angeles, followed by rehearsal. Later that night, Alan's sister called with the news of their father's passing. At rehearsals, the staff and cast immediately rallied around him. Alan recalls how he grateful he felt for their support, and the responsibility of performing in the pageant helped ease the pain.

Diane Freiman Reynolds* plays dual roles in the Glory of Christmas and Easter pageants. She plays Mary and a Shepherdess in the Glory of Christmas, and Mother Mary and Mary Magdalene in the Glory of Easter. She also performs as a courtesy of the Actors' Equity Association.

Diane comes from a musical family. Her mother, Ruth Frieman, directed the Crystal Cathedral's Hand Bell Choir. Little Diane toddled along with her mom until she was 9 years old and could sing in the Cathedral's Girls Choir. Diane performs in numerous musical theater productions, has been on National Tours, and can be heard as a studio singer in movie sounds tracks. Her husband, Royce, sang the part of the blind man for two years in the Glory of Easter production.

One of Diane's greatest joys came when she learned she was pregnant. She was performing as Mother Mary in the Glory of Easter. The following Christmas her infant daughter, Madeline, had her first theatrical debut as Baby Jesus during a curtain call. Since then Madeline, now 8 years old, has been on stage standing beside her mother as one of the shep-

herd children. In one scene Diane, as the Shepherdess, sings the song "Some Children See
Him" to a group of young shepherd children of
different nationalities including her own child.

When daughter Madeline was in third
grade, she was asked by her teacher to create a
story about the most favorite thing she had ever
done. Madeline knew immediately what she liked
best. She drew a picture of the Glory of Christmas
manger with a donkey and a sheep. Underneath
she wrote, "The most exciting thing that I do!"

During one of the performances of the
Glory of Christmas there is the scene where
Diane, as Mary, and Michael Skidgel, as Joseph,
arrived in Bethlehem. There was no lodging
available and they were given a manger with
some straw to rest in for the night. It was time
for Mary, played by Diane, to appear with the infant Baby Jesus. But the baby doll used as a
prop was missing!

Panic set in as the music grew louder. It
was the cue for Mary and Joseph to return to
the manger with the newborn Baby Jesus.
Diane, as Mary, quickly removed her blue shawl
and tried to bundle it like a baby. Together she
and Michael, who was playing Joseph, took her
pregnancy padding and improvised by swaddling
it with her blue shawl. The pad was quite thick
and with the cloth wrapped around it made for a
very large baby. Diane teasingly said, "It re-

sembled a 35 pound toddler more than a newborn baby."

Diane and Michael, in the role of Mary and Joseph, immediately appeared on stage with the make-shift "baby" just in time to sing a verse of "Silent Night." At the same time, some of the women and children ran to the manager to worship the infant Christ Child. Imagine the surprised looks of these cast members when they approached the manger and saw what Diane, as Mary, was cradling in her arms.

Peter Uribe,* also a member of the Actors Equity Association, has performed as Herod in the Glory of Christmas and is honored to play the role of Jesus in the Glory of Easter. It is humbling for Peter to portray the one man who truly has had the most impact on the world.

One evening, Peter, as Jesus, was carrying the cross to the base of Golgotha. He tripped going up the stairs and hurt his knee. Minutes later on the cross during the Crucifixion scene, blood began oozing from his knee and dripped down his leg. Diane, in the role of Mother Mary, looked up and was deeply affected. She felt a mother's pain when she saw real blood flowing from his knee. In that moment she felt as though she was experiencing what it must have really been like for Mother Mary to watch her son Jesus being crucified.

Peter Uribe* is an accomplished actor, director, and teaches at Cal Poly Pomona. His directing talents were also utilized in assisting volunteer cast members in delivering their lines for the latest filming of a Glory of Easter DVD.

The commitment of the professional actors to the pageants does not end at the close of the show. Many of them continue to research and study their characters between shows.

Daniel Bryan Cartmell* is an actor who has spent extensive time studying the historical and political impact of the individuals he portrays. He gains new insight into their characters and values, by incorporating them into the roles he is playing.

Daniel has played Herod Antipas in the Glory of Easter for seventeen years. The first time he was approached to do the part, he was hesitant. He was already portraying a sheriff during the day in another show.

The Actors' Equity Union commented, "You are the only actor in Southern California to have two simultaneous contracts." Daniel rose to the challenge by rehearsing the role of a sheriff by day and playing Herod Antipas, son of Herod the Great, at night. It gave him momentum and before long he was cast as Herod Antipas and Nicodemus in the Easter pageant.

The intensity of Daniel's research took on new dimension when he was also cast in the role of the Rabi and King Herod in the Glory of Christmas. Now he had four subjects to study along with paralleling and comparing those characters with the Roman soldiers, Pilate, the Jewish villagers, and members of the Sanhedrin Court.

Daniel has never been bored playing two very different Herod roles. He admits, "I have played Herod Antipas at Easter in every conceivable way from a screaming maniac, to a lunatic, from a falling-down drunk Herod, to a crazy man.

He continued, "My research has finally captured the essence of Herod as a man who was Half-Jew. Jews do not consider Half-Jews as equals."

"Herod Antipas cultivated his popularity with the Roman leadership and was friendly with Caesar. However, he was not well liked by Pilate because of some religious and political ramifications," Daniel shared with Alan Coates*, who plays Pilate.

What evolved for Daniel was the ability to portray Herod Antipas and show how Herod's contact with Jesus changed even him. The scene occurs in Herod's Court where Herod mocks Jesus during His trial. The verbal exchange between the Rich King/Poor King results in Herod dressing Jesus like a king. By understanding the conflict between the Jews and the Romans, Herod chose to send Jesus back to Pilate.

Together these two actors were able to implement their findings and bring out the political aspect of this conflict in their mannerisms and delivery. (The politics parallel what is going in the Middle East today) These two veteran actors are deeply interested and excited about all the intricacies of their roles. There is a fascination with the history and the politics, which they share with Paul David Dunn, the Producer/Director. They possess a keen desire to deliver their parts with clarity and with impact on the cast and audience. It is amazing how the pageants have held the interest of these veteran actors for almost twenty years.

While waiting in the wings or standing on a stairwell, Daniel humbly reflects, "I am so grateful for this job. I am thankful for every entrance I make, for every opportunity to convey this story."

Daniel also has a tremendous respect for the volunteer ushers and cast members, who have enriched his life. Playing Nicodemus on stage Daniel personally interacts with more of the volunteers when he is not saying lines. He surprised Winnie Herndon, a villager in the marketplace, during a performance when he reached down to assist her exit from the stage. It has become a ritual for them.

Daniel feels fortunate that his cues are spaced so he can get acquainted with some of the volunteers at mealtime between performances. Daniel enjoys hearing about their activities and talents. It also gives everyone an opportunity to get to know him as a person rather than judging him only for the character he plays.

The animals are a major element in the pageants. Daniel's favorites are the camels. Acting in the role of King Herod makes him less than popular with an audience. So he enjoys making his curtain call entrance by kissing the camels and giving them carrots and apples in the process.

Bodie Newcomb,* another member of the Actors' Equity Association, serves as the Production Stage Manager. He is responsible for casting and coordinating all staging activities for more than two hundred volunteers and professional actors. Through the years, Bodie has portrayed eight different characters in the Glory of Christmas and the Glory of Easter and has filled in for other roles in an emergency. He started eighteen years ago when stage manager, Peggy Riley, asked him to audition for the role of the Disciple Thomas. He had only two days notice to prepare when another actor left during rehearsal. Bodies other roles were as the Roman Captain, Herod, Pharisee, Judas, Caiaphas, and for seven years the challenging role of Jesus.

Bodie said, "I went to Catholic school and thought I knew it. But trying to research that all again and convey what I thought I knew, to several thousand people every night, was eye opening."

He continued, "When you are on stage the people around you, especially the volunteers, have such conviction and passion for being there. They are not on stage for a paycheck. They are there because 'it is in their heart'!"

"Performing next to these committed volunteers made me a stronger as an actor and a person. It strengthened my beliefs," Bodie said, "I knew I had to deliver."

Bodie credits another actor, Robert Winley (who passed away from a brain tumor) for being his mentor. Robert was so spontaneous and spiritually present in the role of Jesus on stage. He was the same off stage with the cast. Children would run and flock to him in the hallways off stage, and he would gently take their hands and walk beside them.

Bodie said, "Robert was a genius as a human being and gave himself spiritually and mentally as an actor and as a friend. He laid the groundwork."

Bodie felt fortunate to observe Robert in the role of Jesus and to learn from him on and off stage. Bodie researched every part he played. This allowed him to show their unique character traits with authority and authenticity.

There were a several times during the Crucifixion scene where Bodie had some challenges. He recalls the night when Pilate said," I wash my hand of this man's blood." The Romans flogged

Jesus some more and pushed him back on stage for the next scene.

It was time to go to Golgotha and the cross was not in place for him to carry. Being a professional, Bodie filled the next three to four minutes by crawling around stage in his already weakened condition from the scourging. For Bodie, the wait seemed like hours.

The most difficult physical challenge was the evening Bodie was hanging on the cross when one of the hooks broke that held his wrist in place. He said, "I felt like a rusty gate swinging from just one fastener."

Naturally, it put a lot of strain on his arm and shoulder. The Crucifixion scene is one of the longer scenes so maintaining his balance and keeping both arms in position was rather painful. It caused him to have a very painful shoulder for the next few days.

Another challenge occurred when he climbed off the donkey during his triumphant ride into Jerusalem for the Passover. The donkey stepped on Bodie's robe. He tried to push the donkey's rear torso over so he could free his robe. Herkie, the donkey, retaliated by stepping on Bodie's foot and broke two toes. Bodie hobbled through the remainder of the show. During the next few weeks, he wrapped his toes with brown duct tape so his injury wouldn't show through his brown sandals.

The hand blown chalice, used during the Lord's Supper, tipped over and wine was spilled. Bodie, in the role of Jesus, immediately grabbed the chalice and one of his disciple's arms. The Disciple John was sitting next to him and the sleeve of John's costume became the perfect sponge.

Bodie Newcomb* is a native of Los Angeles and has acted on the stage for more than twenty years. His familiarity with all aspects of productions helps him interact on all levels with the staff and the general cast. Bodie is a trusted friend and favorite with the cast members performing in the pageants

Bodie says, "It is the magnitude of the pageant that continues to impress me." Most theatrical productions involve less than fifty people. These pageants involve a full cast of professionals, an entourage of animals, and literally hundreds of volunteers.

Truly, the most amazing aspect of the pageants for Bodie is the dedication of the volunteers. Bodie says, " It used to baffle me how they always show up every season."

"I don't want to come to expect it, but it is always there," Bodie continues. "Each year new families appear and some of the same people return. All I have to do is make sure the show starts on time."

"It is the volunteers who make the show run," Bodie said, "They make the show click -

like a well oiled machine. Without the volunteers there would be no show!"

After more than twenty-five years, the pageants are still fresh. The performances are never stale. The storyline stays the same, but delivery by the cast and support of an outstanding technical team sharpens the productions to make them even more spectacular each year.

The First Mary

Debby Smith Tebay was singing in a choir at Fullerton College, which was providing the sound track for the first Glory of Christmas Pageant. The sound track was to include three solos "O Holy Night" "Little Drummer Boy" and a lullaby. Debby's director encouraged her to make an audition tape of the lullaby "Sleep, Holy Child." The director was enthralled with Debby's sweet melodic voice, such a contrast to the operatic voices he had been reviewing. He suggested to the producer that they cast Debby in the part of the Virgin Mary.

Debby recalled the first year was more like the "Pageant of the Masters," held in Laguna Beach, California, in which she appeared like a painting of the Madonna wearing a blue glitter-like gown and gold headdress. There were no speaking parts and she had to keep her head down and "lip-sync" the song. She finds the changes that occurred since the first Glory pageant, under the direction of Paul David Dunn, more authentic with Mary taking on a more humble and believable role.

Celebrities such as (Debbie Boone, Robert Goulet, and Carol Lawrence) were cast in some of the earlier Glory of Christmas shows. Jim Nabors was cast as a shepherd the year Debby Smith Tebay was in the role of Mary. They were in the midst of a late night rehearsal. Jim Nabors had just finished singing "O Holy Night." As he knelt at the manger, facing Debby holding the Baby Jesus, he first smiled and then shouted using his "Gomer Pyle" voice, "SHAZAM! It's a Boy!" ending a late night on a humorous note.

One of the most touching moments for Debby, came after one of the Children's daytime shows. Thousands of school children are invited each year and Debby had just completed her third show that afternoon. She was waving and walking down the center ramp with the rest of the cast to the music of "Joy to the World" to go outdoors to greet the children, their teachers, and drivers.

Once outside, Debby noticed a weeping woman, who appeared to be the caregiver, pushing a wheel chair toward her. The passenger was a young girl (7 or 8 years old). The woman's tears glistened and trickled down her pink cheeks as she approached Debby and exclaimed,

"This child has not spoken a word since her parents were killed in a fire a year ago. During your song, she said 'Jesus, Yah, He's the one who held me when my parents died!' "

Greeting the audience has been truly meaningful for Debby. In the role of Mary Magdalene in the Glory of Easter, she has seen the audience in tears and has been approached afterward with comments like "I just had no idea this was the whole story . . . there is forgiveness . . . and hope."

Debby finds the Glory of Easter rehearsals the most wrenching, especially when rehearsal ends before they have time for the Resurrection. Easter is more of a drama. It doesn't make any difference to Debby whether she is in the role of Mary Magdalene or Mary the Mother of Jesus. Both roles require emotions that can be draining. Sometimes rehearsal time runs short and the cast has to be dismissed before they can finish with the good news of Jesus' Resurrection. As cast members the real test of their performance abilities comes in being able to adapt and transfer these emotions, knowing deep within their belief system that it allows them to process their feelings in a positive way.

For Debby, rehearsals took on a new twist after she was married and her children became involved in the pageants. In one of her roles as a Shepherdess in the Glory of Christmas, Debbie came on stage singing "Some Children See Him." The words describe children of various nationalities seeing Jesus in a color identical to their particular race.

To give the scene impact, children of different ages and nationalities gather around Debby as she sings. Debby's son, Jesse, was one of the children, but he wasn't much interested in mom's singing and began amusing himself by doing the "Bunny Hop" on stage. Jesse has matured since then and moved on to becoming the shortest Roman Soldier.

Eventually, Samuel and Amanda joined the cast as children in the market scene. Over the past seventeen years these pageants have evolved into a family activity as Debby Smith Tebay brought the growing of her own family to the Glory.

My personal connection with Debby is that she was the soloist on the Hour of Power television show singing "O Magnify the Lord," on the Sunday morning of my angelic landing as an interview guest of Dr. Robert H. Schuller. (See the cover of this book for a visual of the landing or read the story "It's Not How You Fly, It's How You LAND!")

An Innkeeper's Compensation

A very pregnant Mary (Donal Carol White) was riding the donkey led by Joseph (Robin Buck) down the center ramp of the Crystal Cathedral toward the stage, which was the setting for the starlit City of Bethlehem. They had endured days of traveling while dealing with the elements of the weather and Mary was extremely tired. She was showing signs of exhaustion and was not sure she would be able to continue the journey. Joseph reminded her of the Lord's promise and said, "We must have faith." Somehow, the caring calmness of his voice provided the encouragement and strength she needed to ride further.

They arrived in Bethlehem with thousands of other people all seeking lodging, because they had been required to return to the place of their families' origin for the Roman census. Making reservations in advance was unheard of in Biblical times. So Joseph was getting accustomed to hearing the words "No room at the Inn." By now, the donkey was almost as tired as Mary who was experiencing the early stages of birthing pains. So when Joseph approached the Innkeeper (Al Zultz), he was adamant and informed him that the child could come that very night.

Recognizing Mary's delicate condition, the Innkeepers wife (Trudy Miller) interceded with her husband. He thought a moment and then suggested the cave located next to the Inn. The cave was used as a stable for the animals. Then the Innkeeper offered them some clean straw. Grateful for the kind gesture and without hesitation, Joseph quickly handed Al Zultz, the Innkeeper, his Visa Credit Card!

Imagine the look on Al's face as he tried to stay in character. Joseph quickly turned away from the audience, chuckling to himself, as he led Mary toward the cave and stable of animals, while adding a humorous, modern day touch to one of his numerous performances in the role of Joseph.

While Shepherds Watch

The shepherds' hill for the Glory of Christmas set extends from the base of the stage on the west side of the Cathedral to the top of the west balcony railing. The audience views this expanse of scenery as a hill formed out of rocks with a few sparse trees and tumbleweed. There is a pathway leading to the top of the hill and the semblance of a campfire. Not visible to the audience seated on the main floor are several steps leading up to the balcony railing, which can only be entered from the landing leading up to the balcony level. During some scenes, cast members as shepherds, enter or exit a scene at the top of the hill from these steps. Other times they may enter from the base of the stage and climb up the hill.

Georgia Smith, along with other cast members who were shepherds, was tending the campfire and guarding sheep on this hillside in Bethlehem. The shepherd angel, Elisha Thomas, had just announced the birth of the Savior to the shepherds. A host of flying angels joined her sharing the news with the shepherds by singing,

"Glory to God in the Highest" then they returned to the angel loft. The transition for the next scene was about to begin when Georgia heard the first 'thump.' The sound was Don Christensen's shepherd's staff announcing his arrival at the base of the first set of stairs to the balcony level. He would be arriving on the hill-side in the next 30 seconds.

At the same moment, Georgia noticed a man in a three-piece suit coming toward her. He was looking at his tickets and started climbing the steps leading to the top of the shepherd's hill where Georgia was tending the campfire. Possibly it was her police training and skills that alerted her to the 'intruder' who was about to become part of the pageant. (Georgia worked full time as a Long Beach Police Officer.)

Realizing he was a late arriving guest, Georgia immediately took him by the arm and led him back down the three steps. Then she directed him to the right side of balcony where the audience was seated. She barely moved the unsuspecting 'intruder' off stage before she heard the second 'thump' of Don's staff. Instantly, the spotlight brightened the hillside as Shepherd Don Christensen started down the pathway singing the German Carol "While By My

Sheep." The show went on without a hitch, thanks to Georgia's alert perception. Otherwise, it could have been a startling spotlight moment for the man in the three-piece suit.

One of Georgia's other tasks as a shepherd was to lead a sheep on a scene known to the cast as the Journey to Bethlehem. The Romans had already announced the proclamation that everyone was to be taxed. So villagers from surrounding areas were traveling by foot to the city of their birth. Some took along animals and Georgia had a sheep to lead.

Georgia said, "It never failed, every time I brought my sheep into the lobby entrance of the Cathedral, it would squat and empty its bladder on the carpet." (Fortunately, during load in for the show, a liner is placed between the existing carpet. A new carpet is laid over the existing carpet for the shows and removed later. This helps prevent the Cathedral from smelling like a barnyard.)

Georgia's sheep would also start to "baa" the minute she led it up the center ramp. It would keep "baa—ing" and "baa—ing" during the entire journey to Bethlehem. "The audience would snicker," Georgia recalled, "It was night and the over all setting for the scene was darker. There was thundering and lightning and the sheep would continue to bleat above the noise." Georgia continued, "The minute I left the stage and went outside, the sheep would stop bleating." Her sheep had established a pattern of piddling and bleating, every time Georgia was present.

Through the years, there have been many cast members who have been shepherds. Around the campfire on the shepherds' hill, Sandy Asche, Gary Franken and Carol Whedon would pretend to be cooking mutton stew. They would discuss among themselves the various ingredients and offer servings to the other shepherds tending the sheep. The menu varied with each performance and sometimes it would be crow soup, jackrabbit stew, or a roast piglet. The variety of their chatter kept them in character and gave them insight into the different foods that may have been consumed by the shepherds. It helped them to make each performance fresh and meaningful.

A Disciple's Rescue

At the entrance to the Garden of Gethsemane, Jesus, (played by Robert Miller) said to His disciples, "Wait and pray with me."

Jesus (Robert) continued walking up the steps to a platform to pray alone. The Glory of Easter set is one of the largest indoor sets in the world. It consists of stairs extending upward from the front to the back of the stage. Each step extends the full width of the stage. Halfway up the stairs is a platform with steps surrounding the platform. When Jesus left His disciples to pray alone, the disciples sat down on the steps below the platform and waited.

Jesus (Robert) prayed, "Father, if it is possible, let this cup pass from me. Yet, not as I will, but as you will." After finishing the prayer, He got up and walked down the steps. His disciples were lying on the steps and were fast asleep.

Jesus (Robert) cried out to His disciples, "What? Could you not watch with me even for one hour? Watch and pray." The disciples awaken at His reprimand. Robert, in the role of

Jesus, then leaves His disciples and returns to the garden platform. He continues to pray, "Father, all things are possible for you, take this cup away from me." Jesus (Robert) weeps and continues, "It is not as I will, but Your will be done."

Suddenly, a cohort of soldiers (one of the ten divisions of a Roman legion) bursts into the Garden of Gethsemane. The disciples, who have fallen asleep again, are awakened by the arrival of the soldiers. Vitelius, who is in command of the legion, rides in on a horse. The rest of the soldiers run alongside, carrying torches and spears, ready for battle. Vitelius, realizing this wasn't much of an uprising, says to his fellow soldier Marcus, "This is what they call a revolution?"

By now the disciples were on their feet, facing Jesus while the soldiers with torches and spears crowded around them. Judas followed the soldiers into the Garden, and turned to them, and said, "The one to whom I give our Passover greeting. He's the one."

Judas walked up the steps and stood in front of Jesus (played by Robert) and said, "Teacher, I've been looking for you." Judas proceeded to extend the Passover greeting to Jesus with an embrace and a kiss.

Vitelius shouted, "That's him, seize him." Just as the command was given Bob Carter (playing the role of the disciple Philip) noticed that the shako (large plume) on a Roman soldier's helmet was on fire. Bob quickly approached this hefty looking solider (a football player at a local high school) reached out with both hands, and removed the helmet from an astonished teenager's head. By then, the flame was spiraling up the plume on the helmet. Bob quickly turned toward the East exit and carefully walked off the stage, holding the flaming helmet in his outstretched hands.

The pageant continued on stage with the soldiers arresting Jesus. Bob just kept walking until he was outside and could drop the fiery helmet into the reflecting pond, outside the East exit of the Cathedral. It was apparent that the teenager, playing the part of a Roman solider, moved his torch too close to his illustrious helmet. Bob Carter's keen eyesight, quick response, and concern for the safety of others was in character with the role he was playing in the pageant as Philip, one of Jesus' disciples.

Solon's Joy

Solon Goodson is involved in many different aspects of the Crystal Cathedral ministry. With each task or committee assignment, he finds JOY in sharing and being a part of a team that reaches out and touches others.

At a church service in 1980, Solon signed up to volunteer for the first Glory of Christmas. He has continued to volunteer in both pageants for over twenty years. The Christmas pageant has two casts but the parts Solon played required him to be there every night. Solon admits, "I was frequently exhausted and almost sick by the end of the last show. But I always forgot about that part, when it came time to sign up for another show."

Casting Solon for the Christmas pageants was easy. Standing 6 feet 5 inches, he already has the physique of king. Dressing him in a shiny elegant robe with an exquisitely draped and beaded headdress certainly enhanced his nobility astride a 6-foot camel. His image illustrates what a person might visualize of a majestic sovereign ruler portraying one of the Three Wiseman.

"My first camel was named Mary Lou," Solon said "She was a gentle camel and well behaved." Solon seemed to have a special connection with Mary Lou.

Solon has portrayed one of the Wisemen in hundreds of Glory of Christmas shows. He is accustomed to wearing any one of the bulky headdresses or crowns. The elegant robes are draped over the Wiseman's shoulder with continuous yards of exquisite fabrics of gold, red or blue trimmed with beads and fringe. With all the embellishments, the robes weigh about fifty pounds. Wearing a costume that adds bulk and an extra fifty pounds involves strength and some creative maneuvering.

Near the end of the Christmas pageant the focus of the scene is on Baby Jesus lying in the manger. Mary and Joseph are nearby, filled with praise by the miracle of His birth. The Three Kings, along with their colorful entourages, are all kneeling in front of the manger. Flying angels return to their lofts after sharing their joy to the music of "Hark, the Herald Angels Sing." The volume of the music suddenly diminishes. The cast is frozen in position. Each of the Three Kings has one arm extended toward the Baby

Jesus while kneeling along with their entourages. Joseph is beside Mary. Mary reaches out and extends her arms over the manger as a laser beam streams down upon the Christ Child.

The deep voice of the narrator, Thurl Ravenscroft,* (which is pre-recorded) is heard saying, "He was born in an obscure village . . . No one in history has ever affected our lives so powerfully as this One Solitary Life. This truly is the Glory of Christmas."

The scene ends with the music of "Joy to the World." At this time the cast rises from kneeling for the finale and exits the stage using the center aisle ramp. The animal/trainers take charge of the animals leading them off to the side exits. The Wisemen, along with their entourages, exit according to their designated colors with gold going first, followed by red, and then blue. After they depart, the remaining cast follows.

During one of Solon's recent performances as a Wiseman, he attempted to rise for the finale after kneeling. Instead of standing, he toppled forward onto the floor knocking his red crown and hairpiece askew. Embarrassed after years of successfully performing this role, he quickly regained his balance, ignored his distorted headdress, and led his entourage down the center aisle ahead of the gold king. Fortunately, Solon was not hurt, except perhaps his pride.

Solon also plays the part of a shepherd at Christmas. He admits the costume for that part is simple compared to the time it takes to dress as a Wiseman. In the Glory of Easter, he is the blind man's father wearing another less elaborate costume.

"I have three wives in the blind man's part," boasts Solon, "Winnie Herndon, Trudy Miller and Nan Ducolan." While Trudy has been in the show since its inception, Winnie has had some health challenges. The cast was excited when she returned last season. Winnie's 4 foot 9 inch torso is quite a contrast standing next to 6 foot 5 inch Solon.

For many years, Solon played the blind man's father every night of the show. It was a welcome relief when Terry Visser, Don Eyer, and others began sharing the role.

Solon said, "Leading a blind man has its challenges when animals are involved. There was one evening when Eddie Quiroga* was in the part of the blind man. I noticed the horses had left some rather large droppings near the pool of Siloam, the exact spot where Eddie was to wash his eyes." Solon continued, "I couldn't point to it during the show, because Eddie was supposed to be blind. I quietly alerted him as we walked and was able to maneuver him around it to avoid any embarrassment for either of us."

During Easter rehearsals one evening

Solon was casually conversing during the break with Robert Winley who was playing Jesus that year. (The cast always referred to him as Winn instead of Robert.) Solon was impressed with Winn's ability to focus and acknowledged him for it. (Winn was also dubbed as the 'Biker Jesus" because he rode a motorcycle to the Cathedral and dressed in leathers. He didn't appear on the surface to be someone who could play the part of Jesus. But he won the hearts of everyone in the cast for his portrayal of Jesus.)

Solon asked, "How do you play the same role so convincingly night after night?"

Winn replied, "There are three things to remember as an actor. They are focus, focus, focus!" Solon recognized that Winn was sincere in his comments, which is why his acting is noteworthy.

In the Easter pageant, there is a scene where a heated discussion takes place between the religious leaders and Jesus. To prove himself Jesus, Robert Winley, approaches the blind man's father and asks, "How old is your son?"

Silent, and at a loss for words for a moment, Solon blurts out "Go ask him yourself!" Instead, Solon was supposed to say, "Ask him, he's of age, he can speak for himself."

So focused was Robert Winley, as Jesus, he

didn't even flinch to the change in wording, but continued the scene without any hesitation. Solon realized then the importance of 'focusing' to an actor.

A few years later, Solon had an opportunity to participate in a scene when a professional actor briefly lost his focus. This occurred after King Herod sent Jesus back to Pilate. Pilate was to offer a compromise by releasing Jesus or Barrabas. Instead, the actor playing Pilate somehow lost his focus and omitted the scourging scene and ordered the Crucifixion.

Imagine the panic that occurred when the stage managers heard this actor as Pilate say, "Crucify Him!" instead of "I'll have him flogged." The actor had skipped over an entire five-minute scene. The stage manager and the props team were scrambling to bring in the cross instead of the whip. They were also repositioning the cast to make it appear to the audience that nothing had gone wrong.

In recent years Solon has played a priest in the Sanhedrin Court. The court is located off to the side of the East balcony, 50 ft above the main floor, facing the audience. The members of the Sanhedrin have a fabulous view of the audience and are able to see the tears and feel the audience's reaction during the performances.

"This is what being in the Glory is all about," said Solon, "touching others who come from places like Estonia, Russia as well as Orange County. It just gives me a good feeling!"

In addition to Solon's three wives as the blind man's father, he does have a real wife named, Denise, who is also in the pageants. Denise has been a manger lady, a village person and an usher. There also times when Solon is an usher and sometimes he serves as a stage manager.

Solon's favorite volunteer endeavor, when he is not is the Glory, is being a tour guide at the Crystal Cathedral on a weekly basis. He receives so much joy out of sharing information about the Cathedral and the grounds with others. It also gives him an opportunity to share some of the stories he has gleaned from being a participant in the pageants.

It is amazing how Solon's stories travel. On more than one occasion, I have had friends call me and say, "Venna, we took a trip to see the Crystal Cathedral. It is amazing. The tour guide even told your story, about the flying angel from San Jose that landed on Dr. Robert H. Schuller during his Sunday interview!" What a thrill to hear about the impact a tour guide, possibly Solon, had on them.

Webster's dictionary defines JOY as, "A feeling or state of great delight or happiness."

This is the same joy Solon conveys regarding his participation as a volunteer at the Crystal Cathedral. Solon said, "It gives me a good feeling. It is a JOY!"

*Thurl Ravenscroft is the official Narrator for the Glory of Christmas and Glory of Easter pageants. His recorded words in the pageants have touched millions. He is especially known for his booming voice of Tony the Tiger, narrator for the Pageant of the Masters, and his link with Disney's characters and films. He passed away at the age of 91. (1914-2005)

A Disciple's Audition

For nearly ten years, Robbie Downs was involved with his family, Jim and Connie Downs, in the Glory of Easter and Christmas productions. Some of his childhood friends were also involved. His friend, Terry Parker, was one of them. Terry and Robbie lived in the same neighborhood in Ontario, California, and grew up together. Terry was a troubled boy, trying to cope with his parents' unstable relationship. When his parents divorced, his home life became almost unbearable. He would avoid spending time at home. Instead, he spent a good share of his time at Robbie's house. Robbie and Terry were best friends.

Terry was on the high school freshman cross-country team—a sport he enjoyed. When his grades dropped, his mother emphatically told him he could not be on the track team. It was a comment any parent might make to a child whose grades were falling, but for Terry it was a combination of parental behaviors and disapproval mounting in his mind. Terry met Robbie at school the next day. On the way home, they stopped at a local Carl's Junior Restaurant. Together they played a few pranks, like when they were younger. They blew some straws at the ceiling and tinkered with packets of sugar and ketchup, while they talked. It wasn't long before the manager asked them to leave. They left the restaurant and decided to meet at Terry's house later in the day. Then they went home.

"Where's Terry?" Robbie asked when he arrived at Terry's house later that afternoon.

Terry's little sister was watching television and said, "He's in his room, I can't wake him up."

Robbie went into Terry's room and discovered Terry . . . with a bullet in his head. His mom's small pistol was beside him. Robbie ran across the street and called 911. The police came, but Terry was dead!

The police questioned Robbie as they investigated what happened. At first, the police thought there was a suicide pact between the boys, and Robbie had chickened out. Imagine finding your best friend dead and having to deal with this line of questioning only moments later! Fortunately, the police changed their attitude after getting more information.

It took a long time for Robbie to work through what he had seen, and the horrible loss of this best friend. Many times he would project his anger and frustration onto others. There were times of questioning, wondering what he might have done, how he could have helped. These unsettled feelings led Robbie to audition for the role of Thomas, one of the twelve disciples in the 1993 Glory of Easter.

Robbie's mother, Connie, drove him to the Crystal Cathedral for auditions. She waited during the auditions outside of the assistant director's office. Suddenly, she heard someone yelling at the top of his lungs. It was Robbie, her son. She couldn't understand what he was saying and began to wonder what was wrong. Soon the door opened and Robbie came out beaming and happy.

Connie was confused. "What happened in there?" she asked.

Her son replied, "I was just playing the part, saying Thomas' lines," replied Robbie. "You know the part, Mom. It is after the women return from the tomb to tell the disciples that Jesus rose from the dead. Thomas does not believe them and he says, 'That is impossible, He is dead!' " Robbie shrugged his shoulders and continued, "I just said the lines as I felt them, and I got the part!"

His family later learned from Terry Larson, the assistant director, that it was the loss of his friend Terry Parker, which inspired Robbie to release his emotions into those few lines during the audition. While performing the role of the disciple known as "Doubting Thomas," Robbie visualized his friend Terry. Terry was Robbie's inspiration in the audition and for playing the part. Robbie's experience of seeing his friend dead was similar to Thomas seeing Jesus crucified and put in the tomb. As a result, Robbie gave a convincing performance as Thomas. This was also Robbie's way of letting go of the guilt, hurt, and loss of his best friend. Robbie continued in the role of Thomas for several years. He can still be viewed performing the role of Thomas in the Glory of Easter video, available in the Crystal Cathedral Book, Music, and Gift Center.

During the past few years, Robbie has assumed the role of stage manager for the Roman soldiers. At Easter he performs as Captain of the Guard. At Christmas, he has a similar role and rides a horse into the Cathedral and gives the decree, "By order of the almighty Caesar Augustus, all subjects are hereby ordered to be registered for the census. Registration must take place in the city of your forefathers. All must be counted. All must be taxed. You have 10 days to comply with this decree."

It is the continuous commitment and dedication of individuals, like Robbie that makes the pageants 'come alive' every year.

Connie's Epiphanies

It is common for cast members in the Glory pageants to experience sudden insights into the spirituality of the moment and find personal meaning and identification with what is occurring on stage. This may be an epiphany. For some, it is the manifestation of being in the presence of their Lord and Savior.

In the last scene of the Glory of Christmas, there are animals, wise men and their entourages, dancers and soloists, all kneeling at the foot of manger with Mary and Joseph worshiping the Baby Jesus. The music of "Hark, the Herald Angels Sing" resonates throughout the Cathedral and flying angels come to worship the Newborn King. For Connie Downs, the idea of a little tiny baby being worshiped by those angels was an epiphany. She was awestruck.

"Angels were worshiping this little tiny baby," Connie exclaimed. "It was something so magnificent," Connie said, "Angels were worshiping a seemingly ordinary little baby. In that marvelous moment 'His Holiness' became a reality to me."

Connie's most profound epiphany occurred during the Glory of Easter. She was standing at stage right, holding a fruit basket and watching the Passover week procession. Jesus was riding a donkey down the center ramp. People were dancing and spreading palms leaves in front of Him and singing "Hosanna" during His triumphant ride into Jerusalem.

Connie cried out, "Hallelujah, Praise God! Jesus is coming."

At that same time one of the disciples walked up to Connie, looked directly at her and said, "The Lord is here." That is when Connie felt she had a spiritual awakening.

Connie said, "The rest of the Jerusalem scene and everything happening on stage (from the trashing of the temple to the healing of the blind man) was a blur to me. Instead, I was alone on stage with Jesus."

She continued, "Jesus was talking only to me. Jesus told me He had healed my son Robbie, and my niece, just like He healed the blind man." (Robbie had heart surgery when he was 2 months old and Connie's niece had a blood disease, which could have caused brain damage or death.) Connie was overwhelmed by the presence of the Holy Spirit and the love He showed for her. She was enthralled and amazed at the way God came to show His love, not only for her, but also for her son and niece.

Connie said, "Jesus invaded my heart that evening by taking an entire scene and making it a scene just between the two of us." As Jesus healed the blind man, so He healed Connie's family. Robbie continues to be healthy. While her niece matured more slowly than normal, she now has the capacity to function as a normal adult.

This year, Connie helped with ushering at the last performance of the Glory of Easter. Walking to her car, she overheard a young girl and her mother talking. They were sharing an epiphany they had experienced as cast members. It was delightful to hear their enthusiasm and the intimate details of their revelations. Connie identified with the gratification they gained.

When she heard the young daughter's request, " Mommy, may we do the pageant again?" Connie knew the pageants were in the capable hands of another generation.

Nicodemus is Alive

Chris Blanas was a dedicated volunteer who took pleasure in performing in the pageants. He played a shepherd, an innkeeper, or one of the Three Wiseman in the Glory of Christmas. In the Glory of Easter he was a priest in the Sanhedrin Court. His favorite role was playing the part of Nicodemus. Even when Chris' health was failing, he would somehow manage to trudge up and down the Cathedral steps to be in the cast. He would lie around the house all day, barely able to walk, but would burst forth with delayed energy when he was sharing God's message with the audience as a cast member.

At first Chris' wife, Loella, participated in the general cast, but she preferred ushering to being a cast member. She likes meeting the public, making them feel welcome and hearing their remarks after the performances. When Chris passed away, Loella moved to Texas to be closer to her family. She returns often to house sit or visit friends in the area. If those visits occur during the pageants, her friends sign her up to usher.

After Loella had finished ushering one evening, she left to purchase a gift at the Crystal Cathedral Book, Music, and Gift Center. The last performance of the Glory was still in progress, so the plaza on the campus was mostly vacant. The night air was cool and brisk as she hurried toward the bookstore. Barely inside, she stopped abruptly and stared at the familiar image in front of her. It was Chris!

His distinct voice said, "I must speak with you Master. I am Nicodemus, a member of the priesthood in the Sanhedrin. A number of us wanted to speak with you today in the temple but we were forbidden."

It was when Jesus replied saying, "Yes, how can I help you," that Loella realized what she was actually seeing. It was a television monitor showing the video of the Glory of Easter. Her husband, Chris, was in the role of Nicodemus in the video.

The Bread Lady

Linda de Ambrosio has a vested interest in nutrition and animals. She originally lived in the state of Washington, where she grew up among three generations of loggers. Pancakes, pies, and sugar were consumed daily as a part of her family's eating habits. Linda was barely eleven years old and already weighed 165 pounds. One day at school, she casually told a new friend, "Someday I want to work with whales."

The friend replied, "You already look like a whale." Her friend's remark hurt, but also became a defining moment for Linda. She turned that haunting childhood memory into creating a business for herself in the area of nutrition and wellness.

While coping with some health issues after moving to southern California, Linda met a woman who was involved with nutrition. This woman traveled on the speaking circuit with another motivational speaker, Zig Ziglar, who was scheduled to speak at a Possibility Thinker's

Luncheon at the Crystal Cathedral. Linda immediately signed up to attend. The lunch was served in another building on the campus known as the Arboretum.

After lunch they all walked over to the Crystal Cathedral. To her amazement, the program began with Three Wise Men on "live" camels trailing down an aisle inside the church. Linda's first thought was, "What kind of a church is this, that lets animals inside?" Then she thought for a moment and said to herself, "Wow, this is my kind of church. God always did use animals to get my attention." Without hesitating, she immediately volunteered for the 1984 Glory of Christmas.

Linda chuckles as she tells others, "A camel brought me to church!" In her first Christmas production, she was one of the village people joining in the celebration of the betrothal of Mary and Joseph. She was also in the Magi's entourage worshiping Baby Jesus at the manger. From time to time Linda would usher, when she wasn't in the cast. Christmas 1984 had a real impact on Linda and she admits, "I always thought I believed in God. Participating in the pageant helped me to understand who Jesus really is. I had a personal connection with Him. Jesus actually 'came to life' and that Christmas I committed myself to Him."

After her Christmas experience, Linda was

eager for the Glory of Easter to begin so she could participate. At rehearsals, she noticed that when Jesus sat down to eat the Passover Dinner with his twelve disciples, they were eating pita bread and not unleavened bread.

Linda admits, it is probably a 'health and wellness thing with her.' She believed to be authentic, the bread should be unleavened, and similar to bread baked in Biblical times for the Passover. (Unleavened bread is made without yeast. It remains flat and doesn't rise, since there isn't any fermentation or expansion process.) She volunteered to create a recipe for unleavened bread.

It was during preview night in the Upper Room scene Jesus, (played by Robert Winley) and the twelve disciples were in position for the Lord's Supper. Robert, as Jesus, sits in the middle of a long table with six of the disciples on one side of him and the other six on the opposite side. The lights are dim, a quiet stillness settles upon them. Robert, in the role of Jesus, picks up Linda's homemade unleavened bread with both of his hands. He begins his lines, "This is my body, eat . . ." As he breaks the bread in half, a loud crackling sound echoes throughout the Cathedral drowning out his remaining lines.

"Oops!" exclaims Linda, but she does not give up easily. By the next evening, she has solved the crackling noise dilemma. Her unleavened bread became so popular with the disciples that she baked double batches, so they could have some in their pockets for a snack. Linda was quite content baking fresh unleavened bread for each performance knowing she was adding something nutritious to their diets.

Linda enjoyed sharing the role of Salome in the Glory of Easter with Emily Beaucham, until Emily was old enough to audition and realize her dream of becoming a flying angel. Salome, along with Mary Magdalene played by JoNel Bayen Christensen, was one of the women who helped anoint Jesus' body and prepare it for burial. She also was with the women who went to the tomb on Easter morning.

As Salome, Linda personally experienced the feelings of loss and sorrow. She confided, "It is like going to a funeral. Jesus is someone I love with all my heart and soul. He is more than a beloved family member or friend. The love I have for Jesus in my heart is the greatest of all loves and there I am, anointing His body. It is upsetting. I am sobbing and overwhelmed with sorrow."

What a contrast of emotions it is for Linda, as Salome, to leave the tomb on the eve of the Sabbath and return with the women on Easter morning. As she walked with these women, they discussed options as to who would roll away the stone from the sepulcher? Linda, as Salome was thrilled to have a speaking part. "Why should they help us, they killed him?" she asked, as they arrived at the tomb and discovered the stone had been rolled away.

Envision the women's surprise as flying angel Gayle Carter Carline greets them saying, "He is not here. He is Risen! Go tell his disciples, He is risen from the dead!"

For Linda, being on-stage for the Crucifixion and the Resurrection is like living in that moment in time. She shared, "I went from a feeling of deep sorrow to the awesome joyful experience of witnessing the angels greeting and the message of His resurrection. 'He came to life' (for me) in the Glory of Christmas in 1984 and He was 'brought to life' at Easter."

Another pleasurable adventure for Linda was helping to promote the Glory of Christmas one year in the Hollywood Christmas Parade. The Christmas performances are double cast due to the longer run and multiple evening shows. The red cast performs one night alternating with the green cast. Cast members not performing could volunteer to wear their costumes and walk in the Hollywood Christmas Parade. Roger Williams, Mr. Piano, would ride in the Glory float and convey holiday greetings on behalf of the Crystal Cathedral. Linda really wanted to volunteer, but a recent hip replacement would prevent her from walking the entire parade route.

Imagine her delight when she was asked, "Would you like to be Mary and ride the donkey?" Even though Linda was an experienced horse rider, riding the donkey was a challenge. The donkey would walk about 10 feet, stop, and do a 360° turn throughout the entire length of the parade. Her donkey's behavior amused the crowd watching the parade, as Linda struggled to keep her pillows in place as a pregnant Mary. Linda was aware of what it takes to "break-in" a horse for riding but little did she realize that by the end of the parade she had tamed a donkey!

"Is it I, Lord, Is it I?"

When Dr. Herman Ridder was on the pastoral staff at the Crystal Cathedral, he would direct a short Maundy Thursday play after the last evening performance of the Glory of Easter. The entire audience, cast, and members of the congregation were invited to attend. It was such a spiritually moving experience that people looked forward to it in spite of the late hour (10:30 PM).

The setting for the Maundy Thursday play was the Last Supper using the same table and props from the Glory of Easter set. Dr. Ridder played the role of Jesus and sat, as Jesus did, near the center of the table. The disciples remained in costume and joined him at the table. Dr. Ridder, in the role of Jesus, began the play by saying, "Tonight, one of you will betray me."

Unsure of what their Lord and Master meant the disciples looked at each other and asked "Is it I, Lord, Is it I?

The disciples had an opportunity to stand at the Lord's Table and give a soliloquy. (a speech in a drama in which a character discloses inner-

247

most thoughts) The disciples shared where they lived in the Holy Land, their occupations, and how they came to follow Jesus. Each disciple ended his soliloquy with the question, "Is it I, Lord, Is it I?"

When Judas finished his soliloquy, Jesus (played by Dr. Ridder) excused Judas to do what he had do.

This service was a truly meaningful experience for the twelve men in the role of the disciples. After the disciples finished giving their soliloquies, Dr. Ridder broke bread and gave communion to the congregation and to the disciples.

"Is there anyone else who needs communion?" Dr. Ridder asked.

Then he rose from the table and walked over to the center ramp. He called out again, "Is there anyone else who really needs communion?"

After a long pause, Dr. Ridder continued, "I know one, I know one who really needs communion."

Judas came running in from the back of the Crystal Cathedral up the center ramp. Dr. Ridder, (in the role of Jesus) met Judas half way down the ramp and proclaimed forgiveness for Judas, just as we should forgive those who have hurt us. It was a powerful visual and vocal message of forgiveness as Judas knelt to receive communion.

Closing Night Antics

The closing night of a performance is a time of mixed emotions. There is some relief in knowing things will return to normal but there is also a feeling of sadness. Sometimes cast members want to share feelings or risk a prank or two just for fun.

Antic #1

In a scene near the end of the Glory of Christmas, the trumpets sound. That signals the entrance of the Three Magi riding camels followed by their entourages in elegant costumes of gold, red and blue to the music of "O Come All Ye Faithful." The procession enters from the west side of the Crystal Cathedral and proceeds along the west aisle.

The first camel, led by his trainer, carries King Balthazar, played by Jose Gonzales, (also known as the Gold King). Following the camel is the Gold Kings entourage dressed in gold costumes. The trainer, also in costume, makes a turn and leads the procession in front of the audience and on to the stage. At this point the trainer directs the camel to cush (sit-down) facing the manger. As the entourage kneels the trainer mischievously hangs a sign on the side of the camel facing away from the audience and toward the cast. On the sign is the name "Manny."

The music continues and King Melchoir enters with his entourage following the same procedure. As his entourage kneels, the trainer also places a sign on red king's camel. This sign says "Moe."

The procession ends with the arrival of King Casper. As his entourage kneels another sign appears on the blue king's camel with the name of "Jack." The three owners of the local Pep Boys Auto Store were named Manny, Moe and Jack. The signs "hidden from the audiences view" were a fun way to tease the cast during a last night performance.

Antic #2

Closing night a year later brought forth another attempt to play a prank on the cast. Once again it involved the scene with the Three Magi. Their camels were in cushed position (sitting down). Their entourages knelt behind them. The music of "O Come, All Ye Faithful" diminishes and King Balthazar, played by Solon Goodson, dismounts. A member of the gold entourage straightens his robe and another hands him his gift for the Christ child, a chest of gold, which he presents to Jesus the Newborn King.

King Melchoir, played by Shawn Wilson, follows presenting frankincense. King Casper, played by Eric King, presents myrrh from an ancient spice root. Following the Magi's gifts, a young shepherd child sings the song, "What Can I Give Him?"

This scene builds to the heralding of trumpets and flying angels soaring above the audience to the first verse of "Hark, the Herald Angels Sing" and returning to their angel lofts. The music diminishes and the cast on stage is kneeling quietly, while flying angel, Gayle Carter Carlin, gracefully ascends above them performing her beautyfully choreographed ballet to the second verse of "Hark, the Herald Angels Sing."

Gayle looks down toward the manger and suddenly sees that the camel's lips facing her had been decorated with bright red gaudy lipstick. Women in the cast were smirking, their faces were partially covered by their costumes. Somehow everyone managed to keep a straight face until the scene ended. After it was all over they laughed hysterically.

Antic #3

Everyone has a basic need for recognition. Some need it more than others. King Casper, played by Bob Carter, is known as the blue king. His entourage wears stunning blue costumes and carries lovely matching blue props. Marilyn, Bob Carters wife, leads his entourage on-stage carrying a huge blue feather fan, which is quite elegant and showy. Some of the cast members, throughout the show, always tried to stand next to someone playing a major role. The rest of the cast was well aware of their ongoing need to always be seen. It was not surprising on the last night when one of them pleadingly asked Marilyn, "What do you have to do to carry the blue king's gorgeous big fan?"

Without thinking, Marilyn shrugged her shoulders and replied, "I had to marry him!" Cast members nearby chuckled, since Marilyn and Bob are married to one another.

Antic #4

Mike McClanahan played the role of a Roman tribune in the Glory of Easter. His administrative duties were to protect the interests of Pontius Pilate and carry out Pilate's commands. Caiaphas and the priests of the Sanhedrin decided Jesus should be crucified, but they had no authority to do it. Only Rome could order a crucifixion. So Caiaphas wrote a message on a scroll and requested a scribe take it to Pilate. (In Biblical times a scroll was a piece of parchment used to write on that was rolled on both ends. Scrolls were sometimes used as means to convey a message. These scrolls were generally hand delivered by scribes.)

"Tribune, tribune," yelled the young scribe, "A message from Caiaphas, a message from Caiaphas."

Mike McClanahan, in the role of the Roman tribune, took the scroll and started unrolling it, which he had done at hundreds of performances. Tucked inside the scroll was a large photo of a rather scantly clad calendar girl. A true performer dedicated to his role, Mike managed to maintain his military dignity and proceed with his lines. Once off stage, he burst into laughter, while sharing the contents with fellow cast members.

A couple of years later, Mike opened the scroll again only to find written inside, "Where's the beef?"

Antic #5

In the Glory of Easter the crowd takes Jesus to Pontius Pilate, played by Michael York. Pilate admits he can find no fault with Jesus and neither could King Herod. It was the custom during the Jewish Passover Feast to release one prisoner. Pilate (Michael York) gave the raging crowd the option of releasing the criminal Barrabas or Jesus. The crowd continued to demand "Release Barrabas, Release the murderer Barrabas!"

Pontius Pilate, played by Michael York, found no fault with Jesus and asked the crowd again, still the crowd insisted, "Crucify Him, Cruicify Him!"

Finally, Pontius Pilate requested a bowl of water. Two of his attendants brought the bowl and poured more water into the bowl from the pitcher. When Pontius Pilate (Michael York) reached into the bowl, he saw a goldfish swimming in the bowl. He continued to say his line, "I wash my hands of His death. Order the crucifixion!" At the same time, Michael was nearly ready to crucify the goldfish slipping and sliding between his fingers.

Buddy's Poem
by Buddy Adler (King Herod)

Twas the fourteenth of December and all
through the church,
not a creature was stirring in the Congregation because the Angel was on her perch;

Dr. Schuller's words had his audience in the
palm of his hand,
while the Angel desperately looked for a good
place to land;

As Dr. Schuller looked thru the glass roof
toward the sky,
you could see the Angel coming out of the
corner of your eye;

Dr. Schuller was so happy because he knew
what was to occur,
and just about that time, the eyes of the
Congregation were on her;

I sat there admiring what I wanted to see,
but little did I realize what was to be;

255

The Angel glided gracefully thru the air,
it was wonderful and beautiful for all to
share;

As you looked at her you soon forgot the
cables,
While Dr. Schuller moved about the Pulpit
as he was able;

It was all too real if you let your mind go
free,
and Dr. Schuller's anticipation was filled
with glee;

As the Angel approached the designated
spot,
Unfortunately I realized, there Dr. Schuller
was not;

Suddenly there arose such a clatter,
the Congregation turned to see what was the
matter;

There on the Pulpit the Angel had ascended,
but alas Dr. Schuller's precise timing for the
moment had ended;

There before our very eyes,

Dr. Schuller had disappeared except his legs and thighs;

There the Angel hung in all her majesty, while Dr. Schuller tried desperately to keep his hair tidy;

It was beautifully hilarious to say the least, the Congregation received an unexpected treat;

Finally Dr. Schuller got out from under her dress,
He must have thought to himself, boy what a mess;

It lifted everybody's spirits without fail,
Although Dr. Schuller did look kind of pale;

But if it were so you could not perceive, because Dr. Schuller's poise and good humor got him a reprieve;

His comment immediately after got him a big laugh,
which no one I know of could have surpassed;

As the Congregation left the church and drove out of sight,

I'm sure they realized Dr. Schuller's Positive Thinking gave him his might;

I thought to myself as I pondered what my eyes did see,
that Dr. Schuller is simply one of GOD'S CHILDREN just like YOU AND ME.

Original Poem by a cast member Buddy Adler,(member of the Actor's Equity Association) who played King Herod in the Glory of Christmas

THE GLORY OF ANIMALS

Horse "Tales"

Tale #1

When the Crystal Cathedral was built, a series of fountains was installed stretching from the entry doors to the altar through the center portion of the Cathedral. In preparation for the Pageants, the fountain area is covered to create an elevated platform, which becomes the center aisle. Various cast members and animals enter or exit using this elevated center aisle. Imagine an audience's reaction when a costumed Roman Captain of the Guard, played by PJ Smith, appears riding a white horse as he charges down the center aisle toward King Herod's Court!

King Herod's Court is located almost level with the East balcony in front of the jumbotron, which is used at Sunday services to project hymn verses and close-ups of individuals participating in the service. For the Glory pageants, the Jumbotron is covered to resemble the balcony of the king's palace.

At one Glory performance Buddy Adler*, as King Herod, was on the balcony with three of his wives and Robbie Downs, his scribe. As King

Herod leaned forward and waited, the Captain of the Guard, PJ Smith, was charging in on his white steed. It was clear that PJ's horse had not slowed his pace. Instead of stopping on stage, the horse was spooked somehow and started going round and round in a full circle. PJ began shouting out his greeting to King Herod " H . . . A . . . I . . . L . . . G . . . R . . .R . . . R" trying to keep his head turned in the direction of King Herod. Somehow, PJ managed to slow the horse's pace and continued his line "Hail, Great King! Wise Men from the East are coming in search of the New Born King." The horse was persistent in circling during King Herod's reply and their exchange of lines.

PJ's primary concern was to keep his horses 360 degree maneuvers from getting too close to the edge of the stage and falling into the lap of someone in the audience, while still delivering his lines in the allotted time. PJ's wife, Georgia, was watching from the shepherd's hills where she and other cast members knew this was not a part of the act. Later, off-stage, Buddy told PJ that was the best "H . . . A . . . I . . . L" greeting he had ever received as King Herod!

Tale #2

There is a scene where the Captain of Guard rides a horse down the center aisle of the Crystal Cathedral into the City of Nazareth bearing a decree from Caesar Augustus stating everyone is to be taxed. Confidently, PJ Smith, as Captain of the Guard, mounted a black horse that evening instead of his usual white stallion. As he rode down the center aisle into the City of Nazareth, he pulled back on the reins and his horse started backing up. The more he pulled back on the reins the more the horse kept backing, and the horse continued backing across the stage with each yank on the reins. Something was wrong!

PJ quickly realized his lines regarding taxation would not have any impact if his horse continued to back away from the village people, who were supposed to react to the urgency of the taxation. So he let up on the reins, dismounted, and led his horse forward, delivered his lines, and continued leading his horse offstage.

Upon returning his horse to the trainer at the end of the scene, PJ learned this particular horse had been trained for calf roping. Whenever PJ pulled back on the reins, the horse was trained to back up to keep tension on the rope between the calf and the horse. This type of training was great for a rodeo but did create a challenge for PJ who managed to take charge of the situation. It was incidents like this one that kept the cast alert and amused in responding to the various unpredictable animal behaviors during each performance.

Tale #3

Front row seating is often the preference of many theater attendees. However, the sets for the Glory of Christmas and Easter performances are the largest in the world and the best seats are a few rows back. Also, the live animals can provide an atmosphere that is unmatched at times.

At an Easter show, some of the cast members on stage were observing the enthusiasm being exchanged by two couples, who were ecstatic about having seats in the very front row. It was evident their enthusiasm reflected on the cast as they began moving into their positions for the Temple scene.

It was the beginning of Holy Week and the Temple in Jerusalem was buzzing with tables of moneychangers doing business with the village people selling sheep, doves and other wares. By order of Pontius Pilate, two Roman soldiers on horseback were on stage facing the temple, with their backs to these two couples. The soldiers were sent to observe and kept order.

Two of the villagers, Marilyn Carter and Loella Blanas, were selling garlic when they noticed one of the soldier's horses starting to lift its tail. It was evident to them what was coming next as they saw the eyeballs of the two couples in the audience expand to the size of golf balls. Within seconds, the horse casually dropped a huge melon-sized load, plopping it on the floor directly in front of the toes of these two couples.

At that moment, Marilyn and Loella were thankful their authentic costumes had pieces of cloth covering their mouths, which helped them stay in character. It wasn't long before an odor erupted adding more authenticity to the dilemma. Once the scene ended and the horses exited the stage, a costumed "pooper scooper" arrived rescuing the two couples from having to endure the remainder of their evening in horse barn surroundings.

(Moral of the story: Think seriously about ordering front row tickets when animals are involved.)

Tale #4

Glenn Grant has his own horse "tale." The actor playing Marcus, a Roman soldier, was sick. Glenn, one of the stage managers, was asked to substitute for the evening's performances. Glenn obliged and came in early that afternoon to learn the lines and practice riding the horse on and off the set, so they would become accustomed to each other.

In the Glory of Easter marketplace scene,

Marcus, played by Glenn Grant as the Roman soldier, was to ride his horse from the back of the Cathedral up the center ramp to the stage. The key to riding a horse up the ramp is being able to duck low enough to clear the area under the balcony.

During the afternoon practice, Glenn was not wearing a costume. Unfortunately, that evening he was wearing a large heavy soldier's helmet with large feather plumes. The helmet caught the edge of the balcony when Glenn ducked. It then rolled and fell against the side of the horse. The horse lunged forward, exposing Glenn's ponytail flowing in the wind, as they rode toward the stage. (Imagine a pony tail on a Roman soldier.)

Suddenly, the horse stopped and started backing up. Then one of the horse's back legs slipped off the ramp and the horse fell to the floor with his rider, still attached. Fortunately, the horse was up on his feet again and Glenn tried to coax him to jump back up on the ramp. At that same moment the horse's trainer appeared and took charge of the horse. Glenn simply dismounted directly on to the ramp, walked forward and said his lines to complete the scene.

After they left the stage everyone was asking, "How's the horse? Is the horse alright?"

Glenn was a bit puzzled, "What do you mean is the horse OK, how about me?"

Tale #5

In Nazareth, the village people were going busily about their daily chores. Laura (La La) Martinez was grinding the grain. Jennie Story was carrying a basket of fruit. (Jennie is also a creative seamstress. She delights in making dolls wearing costumes similar to those worn by the cast.) Children were running and playing. Others in the village were tending to the animals. It appeared to be a typical day in the village.

Suddenly, the music swelled and the Captain of the Roman Guard (Fred Booher) rode a powerful white stallion down the center ramp of the Cathedral. The stallion's gait on the ramp caused the horse to somehow lose his balance. Suddenly, the stallion tripped and fell into the aisle landing on his stomach. The prospect of a large stallion falling on them had people near the aisle move immediately out of their seats and away from the ramp. Ironically, people in wheel chairs were also scrambling out of their seats. Fortunately, everyone was safe and unhurt. Through it all, Fred stayed calm and in control, mounted on his horse throughout the fall. He immediately coaxed the stallion to a standing position and back on to the ramp to complete the taxation scene. A dedicated volunteer Fred demonstrated the philosophy of an actor — "The show must go on!"

Horse Tale Tribute

Michael McClanahan was admired and respected by cast members for his dedication and commitment as a volunteer in the Glory of Christmas and Glory of Easter productions. Mike was cast in the role of the Captain of the Guard. His powerful physique matched his character as he road a horse onto the stage each time. He also took the responsibility of stage manager for the Roman soldiers. During his tenure as stage manager, Roman soldiers under his command knew where they were to be and what to do both on and off the stage.

When Mike learned he had cancer of the esophagus, he provided detailed directions to his stage manager/soldier replacement. Cast members rallied around him. They prayed and visited him in the hospital during surgery. After chemotherapy, Mike returned to the cast and performed in one more pageant. Although he was much thinner and weaker, he managed to mount his horse and deliver his lines. Mike's presence truly inspired the Glory cast. After the production ended, God had other plans for Mike. Perhaps Mike is riding another horse in the army of the Lord.

Animal Antics

Camels have a reputation for spitting. Ushers and cast members experience a direct hit from time to time from camel spit. These animals are large, over 6 feet tall, and strong. When cast members stand too close or startle a camel, the camel will spit or butt up against them. The camels sometimes caused a bruise or two depending on the sensitivity of the individual. BJ Scheid recalls an encounter with a camel that created a bruise reaching from her elbow to the top of her armpit.

King Balthazar, played by PJ Smith, was riding his camel off stage toward the East exit. An audience member unexpectedly stood up in front of them and took a flash photo. The flash frightened the camel who immediately reared up from behind and lunged forward.

PJ realized they were only inches from the balcony overhang. He quickly ducked his head lower than usual and barely slipped under the balcony overhang. PJ's quick thinking saved his kingly head. The crown of jewels and embellishments he wears makes him 12 inches taller and

269

adds extra pounds to his body mass. PJ managed to escape unscathed, except for losing his moustache. ("No Flash Photography" signs have a significant meaning for PJ.)

Imagine a child soloist competing with a bleating lamb. The minute the child started to sing, the lamb starts bleating. It becomes a duet between the lamb and the child soloist. When she stopped singing, the lamb stopped bleating. Perhaps it was the pitch of this particular soloist's voice that caused the lamb to bleat in harmony. Who knows?

Shepherd Ann Creager and Bob Van't Hof led sheep in during the Glory of Christmas for several different scenes. In between scenes, they would stand near a corner in the Cathedral behind the curtain waiting for their next cue. Ann noticed one evening that her sheep was not interested in walking very far or even moving very fast. Obviously, the sheep was pregnant.

Concerned about the sheep's delicate condition, Ann asked Bob," What do you think, is this sheep alright?"

Bob replied, "I don't think it is a concern yet, but ask the animal/trainer."

So Ann approached the animal/trainer and asked, "Is it wise to continue taking this sheep on stage? She is making strange noises."

The animal/trainer replied, "The sheep is probably in the beginning stages of labor, but it shouldn't be a problem."

So Ann slowly coaxed her sheep on stage for the adoration scene. This is the time when the humble Mary, played by Donal Carol White Meeks sings "Sleep, Holy Child" to her new Son. It is a quiet scene and the focus is in on Mary and Baby Jesus. No one is to talk. At the same time, Ann's sheep went down on its knees and started making more strange sounds.

Ann whispered to Bob, "We better get her up."

Bob, who never talks during a quiet scene, whispered back, "No, I think she is OK."

Ann responded, "What happens if she has the lamb?"

Bob replied, "If this is Bethlehem, and it is, then that is just what would happen."

Ann continued, "We can't have her give birth on stage."

Bob said, "Oh, don't worry." But then the sheep rolled over on her side and started making even more strange noises.

Bob finally reacted and said to Ann, "This must be for real. Can you get her off?"

Bob helped Ann lift the sheep up on her hind legs. Ann took the ewe down the ramp and gave the sheep to the animal/trainer. He took the sheep to Animal Land in the Cathedral parking lot. Before the cast left for the evening, they learned that the ewe had given birth to twins!

Lambs are usually born in the springtime. What could be more normal during the Glory of Easter than to have the ewe give birth. As a stage manager, unless they have been around animals, having the ewe suddenly lie down on stage can be an eye opener. These situations have occurred more than once during a show. Ewes have even been known to give birth on the grass adjacent to the Cathedral while the show's in progress.

One evening, the production stage manager simply stopped the show for a few minutes when the ewe started birthing on stage. An announcement with the reason for the delay was given to the audience. It was only a matter of minutes . . . until the show continued. The next evening a proud young cast member cradled the newborn lamb in his arms and walked across the stage with the lamb's mother following closely behind.

Sheep are not very cooperative when bridled with a rope. If the baby lambs run free, the mother will go wherever her baby goes. Lambs are quite playful. Sometimes they jump off the ramp, run into the audience and back up on stage again. One evening Melani Wacker, (Lani) was leading the ewe following her week old lamb.

The lamb pranced about and then suddenly leaped off stage. Lani was practically in a spread eagle position on the floor, when her sheep suddenly jerked the rope to dart after her lamb. At the same moment the lamb jumped back up on stage easing Lani's concern.

It really doesn't make any difference what the cast is doing on stage when the young lambs are prancing about. The audience's attention is completely focused on these adorable creatures and their antics, which only enhances the nostalgia of the pageant. They are so innocent and precious, it is understandable why God would call His followers "His lambs."

Some of the cast members admit they used to enjoy having lamb chops for dinner. But after being in the pageants they have lost their appetite for lamb. They recall their joy in watching the lambs prance about the stage often upstaging the dancers with their grand jetès'. (long horizontal jumps)

Marilyn Carter enjoyed her role as a manger lady at Christmas. She especially liked the goats. Her favorite goat was named Nanny. It was a red nanny goat. (A nanny goat is a female goat.) Nanny was so well trained she could walk without a leash. Marilyn soon learned that goats wanted to eat all the time. Her goat would try to eat parts of her costume and was constantly nibbling the tumbleweed that adorned the stage sets. Marilyn secretly wondered what fun it would be to have a goat farm.

On a trip to the San Juan Islands several years later, Marilyn and her husband Bob Carter happened upon a road called "Carter Lane." It was only natural for them to follow it. Much to Marilyn's delight "high on a hill was a lonely goat herd." It was a combination of the lyrics from "The Sound of Music" and memories of her Glory experiences. In the pasture, were several herds of goats grazing. Marilyn's secret longing for a goat farm became a photographic opportunity while on a drive on "Carter Lane."

In the Glory of Easter, there is a scene where Pontius Pilate could find no fault with Jesus. Realizing Jesus was a Galilean, Pilate knew that Galilee was King Herod's jurisdiction. So Pilate sent Jesus to King Herod for questioning. In this scene, King Herod is in the midst of a glorious celebration with food and wine and elaborately clad dancers in his courtyard.

Adorning King Herod's courtly surroundings and adding to the festivities are two live peacocks perched on stands on either side of King Herod. What an impact the peacocks have during a performance when they spread their gorgeous tails.

Prior to the beginning of the scene the stage

manager made a radio call to Animal Land to bring the peacocks. When the animal/trainer noticed one of the peacocks had unexpectedly died, he immediately got on the radio and said, "We have one dead peacock, what do you want us to do?"

Terry Larson, the assistant producer, was known for his sense of humor and quick wit for keeping things moving quickly responded, "Bring the dead bird!" The animal/trainer took him seriously and before anyone else could respond, one live bird and one dead bird appeared on stage. The trainer stood beside the dead peacock, propped up its lifeless head and helped it appear normal until the end of the scene. It was a lifeless performance!

A stunningly beautiful white stallion is in the show and every time this horse would step inside the Cathedral lobby, he would spray the carpet. The horse looked so majestic clopping through the parking lot from Animal Land. Once inside the Cathedral, it became the stallion's nightly ritual to empty his "gift" into the carpet bringing chuckles from the ushers. The audience was totally unaware of the ritual, but the stallion's performance on stage could merit an Oscar nomination.

One evening, the white stallion was substituted for another horse in the Glory of Christmas. Tony Williams, in the role of the Captain of the Guard, would ride the new horse down the center ramp toward King Herod's Court to announce the pending arrival of wise men coming from the East.

Tony's horse began galloping down the center ramp and just kept on galloping past King Herod's Courtyard. Tony quickly ducked his head to clear the East balcony over hang. The horse continued galloping until he was off stage and stopped at the East exit. It all happened so fast that Tony was delivering his lines off stage and out of sight of the audience.

King Herod, played by Buddy Adler*, was watching the Captain of the Guard, (Tony) gallop past his elevated Courtyard. Usually in a stern and rigid stance during the scene, King Herod (Buddy) had all he could do to keep from doubling over in laughter. After that experience, each time Tony and Buddy passed one another in the lower concourse one of them would say, "Whoa . . . Horsey Whoa!"

During the Glory of Christmas, a little tiger cub was added to King Herod's Courtyard. Three wise men on camels arrive at King Herod's palace seeking knowledge of a newborn baby, who is the King of the Jews. King Herod, played by Buddy Adler*, is holding and petting a little tiger cub, named Tazz. The baby tiger starts purring and with each stroke, Tazz's purring response grows more intense. The baby cub's purring begins to sound like a growling stomach over the microphone and completely drowns out King Herod's (Buddy's) attempt to converse with the wise men. The audience is laughing at the little tiger cub's ability to upstage the actor.

When Tazz wasn't growling, he was chewing on King Herod's (Buddy's) hand. According to King Herod (Buddy) Tazz was a cute little cub, but he had some sharp teeth and one evening blood started dripping down Buddy's hand to the floor below the courtyard. After that King Herod (Buddy) wore a leach (big black leather glove) to save his hand from being chewed.

During the week of technical rehearsals, the Cathedral is closed to tours at various times of the day in order to rehearse the animals. The music played during these rehearsal times helps accustom the animals to the sounds and noise, while some of the animals are led through the cathedral. This is especially important when working with the larger animals like the camels and horses. Linda Booher tells of a day when the animal/trainer was rehearsing with the 350-pound Bengal tiger. The tiger added intrigue to Pontius Pilate's court located on the East balcony of the Cathedral.

Linda is also a tour guide at the Cathedral. She apologized to the group she showed around the campus that day and said, "I'm sorry we can't go inside the Crystal Cathedral today. The

Cathedral is closed for training inside, because the tiger is in there rehearsing." One of the tourists in her group remarked, "I always heard Dr. Schuller was dynamic, but I didn't realize you called him a tiger!" Linda laughingly explained it was a live four-legged Bengal tiger rehearsing inside the Cathedral.

Unpredictable behaviors of the animals add intrigue and uniqueness to the pageants, making each performance vulnerable to sudden change or focus. Their antics range from charming the audience to challenging the cast to step around the "gifts" they leave behind. The animal involvement is a welcome addition to the pageants. The special events coordinator, Jim Downs, categorizes it best with his greeting, "Welcome to the Crystal Barnyard!"

THE GLORY OF GIFTS

"Open to Buy"

Walking into the Crystal Cathedral Book, Music, and Gift Center is a glorious sensory shopping experience. The retail staff has created enticing displays of Christian books, music, gifts, and unique merchandise just begging to be bought. "Open to buy" is a buyer's term indicating the stores owner or buyer has a budget and are ready to place an order. After attending the Glory of Christmas or Glory of Easter pageant, this store is the place to visit to find the perfect remembrance of the most spectacular events ever portrayed. You, too, will be "open to buy."

In 1977, Jim Webb opened the first Crystal Cathedral Book, Music, & Gift Center across the street from the Crystal Cathedral on Chapman Avenue, in what is now known as the Kaiser Building. Pastor Bud Pearson assisted for three months before taking over the Singles' ministry from Pastor Jim Smoke. Jim Webb said, "His goal was to purchase things that provided a Christian witness and were relevant to the Cathedral."

Jim's greatest joy, while managing the store,

was meeting people who had come to the store from around the world. Art Fleming, from the television show "Jeopardy" was a frequent visitor and a mail order client, making it another aspect of the store's business. Jim recalls visiting in depth about the mechanics of operating a bookstore with an inquisitive young pastor attending the Institute for Successful Church Leadership. That pastor was Rick Warren, whose church currently has thirty thousand people attending their services.

Assisting Jim in the bookstore were Malinda Sterbling and Pam Weber. Malinda assisted with the buying. They were constantly ordering and setting up book tables for various conferences. Keen on merchandising, they decided to hang half a dozen shirts with Crystal Cathedral emblems in different locations at various heights from the store's ceiling. Customers could see them easily and sales on t-shirts started booming. One day Dr. Robert H. Schuller walked into the store, looked up, and exclaimed, "What is this a Chinese laundry?"

During the Glory of Christmas the store was open for thirteen hours a day, when Jim was manager. Jim opened the store and stayed until closing during the 33 days of the Christmas pageant. Staffing and relocating the store were always challenges. During Jim's eighteen years of managing the store, it moved from its original location across the street to the youth center and finally to the fellowship hall on campus. Each move made it more accessible to those attending the pageants.

My business relationship with the buyers of the Crystal Cathedral Book, Music, and Gift Center began during the time I was a flying angel volunteer. After two years of coping with a hectic commute schedule from my home in San Jose for rehearsals and performances, I resigned from my Personnel Specialist Recruitment position for two colleges, just before the flying angel Easter auditions with no guarantee of being selected. Was that a "leap of faith?"

Searching for a new line of work, I attended the Los Angeles Wholesale Gift Show. I was drawn repeatedly toward booths that contained items with 'wings.' Inspired and influenced by my desire to continue to be a flying angel, I became a manufacturer's representative in the wholesale gift industry, selling only product lines that contained angels. It was a risky decision. Angels were not popular then like they are today. Retailers only sold angels at Christmas. I convinced myself this was a way to continue to audition to be a flying angel volunteer, and ease my commute. I would establish a client base and sell angels to different retail stores, while traveling between Northern and Southern California for rehearsals and performances. The Crystal Cathedral Book, Music, and Gift Center was one of my early clients and Jim and Malinda bought some of my lines of angels.

Sales were slow at first. It was difficult finding manufacturers with angels in their product lines. It was an even greater challenge convincing retailers to sell angels year around. My flying angel experiences became my sales tool. It gave me an opportunity to promote the pageants while I generated sales. It wasn't long before I became known internationally as the "angel lady rep" in the wholesale gift industry.

By then I was responsible for a trade show booth at the San Francisco and Los Angeles Wholesale Gift Shows. In need of sales support for the Los Angeles show, I asked Malinda Sterbling to sell. Malinda was also the ideal person for me to hire. She had sales experience and lived in the area. She also benefited as a buyer, since she could observe first-hand, which angel items were the best sellers at the show.

My transition to working with the bookstore's next set of buyers, Katy Marcotte and Lori McCoy, went smoothly. Katy had been a buyer for Grace Cathedral's Gift Shop in San Francisco and Lori was a buyer at Knott's Berry Farm's Gift Shops. We already had established relationships, since they carried some of my lines in their previous gift shops.

Relocating from San Francisco and assuming the buyer's role at the Crystal Cathedral was a natural for Katy having been the manager/buyer for Grace Cathedral's Book, Music, and Gift Store. Katy said, "I look forward to the opportunity of taking a store that has potential and making it more than a store. I believe it should fill the needs of people searching for quality up-to-date Christian books, music, and unique gifts. To be a part of expanding the shop's location provides wonderful opportunities for ordering new and different merchandise."

Teaming up with Katy in this endeavor was Lori McCoy. Lori started working part time and became the manager of the Crystal Cathedral Book, Music, and Gift Center in 1995. Katy recalls one of their first mutual projects in revamping the store started with a suggestion when Katy said," Let's move the greeting cards away from the window."

Lori replied, "Can we do that? Will it be OK?"

"Sure it will!" Katy replied, "You are the manager and we can do it." That was the beginning of moving things around to create a new look for the store.

When the construction began for building the International Center for Possibility Thinking, the store was moved again to a large tent. Lori

McCoy was on the committee that helped design the store's present location in the International Center—a wonderful place where everyone is welcome to browse and buy.

Book signings following Sunday Services and during conferences are an on-going occurrence for Lori's capable staff. The famous Italian Fontanini Collection was featured for three years during the Christmas season. Fontanini's grandson and president of the one hundred year old company came to sign the company's lovely hand painted pieces.

Creativity is in abundance when Lori and her display team incorporate interesting ways to display different items of interest for children, special event happenings at the cathedral or even collectibles from various artists. Lori McCoy is the current Manager/Buyer with a creative staff, willing to help anyone needing assistance who is "open to buy."

Acknowledgements:

Dr. Robert H. Schuller, Inspirational Mentor
Paul David Dunn, Producer/Director
   Glory of Christmas, Glory of Easter
Emily De Shazo, Editor and Encourager
Claudia Holloway, Photographer
Catharine Foresman, Graphic Designer
   Purple Cat Productions
Tony Bishop, Technical Support
Alex Morgan, Layout & Design Support
Bill DeHart, Publication Support
Lowell D'Arcy & Phyllis Stiles, 'Angelic'
   Motivators

"Glory Stories" was a joyful undertaking because of the enthusiastic support and encouragement you provided. I thank you for your time, your inspiration, and your guidance. YOU are the Glory Story and this is YOUR book! I was merely the joyful storyteller.

   Arthur (Buddy) Adler*, Erica Anderson, Angel Asche, Emily Asche, Fred Asche, Sandy Asche, Stephanie Asche, Tiffany Asche, Bradley Baker, Herbert Baker, Emily Beauchamp, Bridgette Bentley, Kathy Black, Chris Blanas, Loella Blanas, Marilyn Blum, Fred Booher, Kasey Booher, Kelly Booher, Linda Booher, Sandy Boselo, Richard Bostard, Nancy Bowman,

Christine Brown, Richard Brown, Rose Brown, Robin Buck, Johnnie Carl, Gayle Carter Carline, Bill Carr, Cynthia Carraway, Doug Carraway, Jessica Carraway, Bob Carter, Marilyn Carter, Daniel Bryan Cartmell*, Kristy Cavinder, Don Christensen, JoNel Bayen Christensen, Alan Coates*, Jacquelyn Coffey, Patrick Couchois, Danny Cox, Sharon Crabtree*, Karen Crane, Ann Creager, Aaron Daly, Ian Daly, Cecilia Dangeil, Teresa Dangeil, Linda de Ambrosio, Jill Holloway Delany, Gary DeVaul, Sheldon Disrud, Cathy Dixon, Mary Joy Dollente, Connie Downs, Diana Downs, James Downs, Jimmy Downs, Robbie Downs, Sarah Downs, Kay Drake, Nan Ducolan, Jeanne Dunn, Tanya Durbin, Debbie Eldridge, Don Eldridge, Tony Elevi, Geri Enderle, Mauro Estrada, Tony Ewing, Don Eyer, Richard K. Faucher, Eula Fluckey, Jim Fluckey, Peter Foy, Fred Frank, Gary Franken, Ruth Freiman, Robert Garrett, Lisa Goering, Solon Goodson, Brian Gould, Jeff Gould, Kaylee Gould, Glenn Grant, Larry Grossman, Ben Hadley, Jack Hadley, Perry Halford, Julia Hara, Rita Hara, Nevin Hedley, Rick Helgason, Winnie Herndon, Dick Higgins, Ruth Higgins, Bruce Hollenbeck, Eric Hornbeck, Scott Hornbeck, Sharon Hunter, Lindsey Imler, Gina Inhelder, Ken Inhelder, Patti Inhelder, Gary Iverson, Bob Jani, Marge Kelley, Bob Krogstead, Daniel Lane, Linda Lane, Robby Lane, Gary Larson, Margit Larson, Terry Larson,

Tom Larson, Cathy Leestma, David Lewis,
Charles Lisanby, Katy Marcotte, Mary Martin,
Laura (LaLa) Martinez, Nick Martinez, Bruce
Martz, Daniel Martz, Kelly Martz, Tammy Martz,
Randy Masoner, Louis Massengale, Dorie Lee
Matttson, Sharon Mayer, Michael McClanahan,
Lori McCoy, Jan Wacker McCurry, Donal Carol
White Meeks, Eugene Mendoza, Jennifer
Mendoza, Landon Christopher Mendoza, Don
Miller, Joel Miller, Kevin Miller, Trudy Miller,
Robert Miller*, Carol Schuller Milner, Coty
Miranda, Sandie Morgan, Bodie Newcomb*,
Juliet Noriega, Katherine (Kitty) Paladin, Cindi
Palomarez, Äida Pardini, Joe Pardini, Terry
Parker, Lois Pearson, Pastor Bud Pearson, Brian
Pereboom, Lisa Pereboom, Penny Pereboom,
Wayne Pereboom, Michael Peterson, Michael
Peterson, Pat Peterson, Suzanne Peterson,
Xavier Peterson, Edward Quiroga*, Thurl
Ravenscroft, Derek Resch, Nikki Resch, Shan-
non Resch, Madeline Reynolds, Royce Reynolds,
Diane Freiman Reynolds*, Dr. Herman Ridder,
Peggy Riley, Penny Salisbury, Betty Scheer, Cord
Scheer, Dalvin Scheer, LeNora Scheer, Barbara
Scheid, BJ Scheid, Arvella Schuller, Dr. Robert
A. Schuller, Barbara Schulz, Beverly Schulz, Ted
Schulz, Lee Sevig, Kris Silver, Michael Skidgel,
Pastor Jeff Slack, Georgia Smith, Pat Smith, PJ
Smith, Pastor Jim Smoke, Malinda Sterbling,
Jennie Story, Heidi Inhelder Strickler, Mark

Strickler, Priscilla Sullivan, Fred Swann, Amanda Tebay, Debby Smith Tebay, Jesse Tebay, Samuel Tebay, Mark Thallander, Kathy Thibodeau, Elisha Thomas, Frank Tillou, Susan Tillou, Roger Tirabassi, Carl Treen, Norman Tuck, Ryan Turley, Peter Uribe*, Debbie Zubiate Van Dyke, Tony Van Dyke, Bob Van't Hof, Terry Visser, Melani (Lani) Wacker, Alan Wagner, Aundrea Wagner, Sonja Wagner, Philip Ward, Nancy Warshaw, Emilie Schultz Webb, Jim Webb, Pam Weber, Gail Wenos & Ezra, Carol Whedon, Heather Whitestone, Ginny Wilfhart, Roger Williams, Tony Williams, Cory Williamson, Kelly Williamson, Kyle Williamson, Robert Winley*, Marcia Worthington, Zig Zigler, Irene Zubiate.

*Member of Actor's Equity Association

About the Author

Values + Vitality = Victory

Venna Bishop is a creative motivational speaker, team building facilitator, and an energetic writer. She revitalizes the character & values of organizations while inspiring teamwork to attain victory.

Venna wrote "Glory Stories" to acknowledge and pay tribute to the hundreds of volunteers, cast and staff members who bring the glorious Gospel message to all. Her research gave the volunteers and staff members the opportunity to recapture meaningful experiences and moments of joy. "Glory Stories" reveals the details of behind the scenes contributions people made while working together as a team.

With sparkling vision, Venna gives presentations that achieve results for businesses, government agencies, associations, non-profits and churches. She frequently is a guest on radio talk shows, a pulpit guest on the *Hour of Power*, featured in an ABC-TV special, and is a member of the National Speakers Association.

Venna Bishop is an award winning author and poet. She is a contributing author in various books and magazines. Venna was selected by the San Jose Mercury News and Woman's Fund as a 2001 Woman of Achievement.

Pos I Publishing

Order Form

Fax orders: 408-725-0218. Send this form.
Telephone orders: Call 800-995-8099
e-mail orders: <u>VennaBishop@venna.com</u>
Postal orders: Venna's Voice 1192 Hyde Ave.
　　　　　　　San Jose, CA 95129-4027 USA

Name: _____

Address:_____

City_____ State_____ Zip_____

Telephone _____

email address:_____

　　　　Copies_____ @ $13.95 each =_____

Sales tax: Please add 8.25% for products
　　　　shipped to California addresses _____

Shipping & handling $5 first book
　　　　$3 each additional book _____

　　　　　　　　　　　　TOTAL_____

Payment: Check   or   Credit Card   Visa

Card Number_____

Name on Card_____Exp.date___/___

_____Check if you want Venna as a speaker.
_____Check to be added to an email list.

Pos I Publishing

Order Form

Fax orders: 408-725-0218. Send this form.
Telephone orders: Call 800-995-8099
e-mail orders: VennaBishop@venna.com
Postal orders: Venna's Voice 1192 Hyde Ave.
                 San Jose, CA 95129-4027 USA

Name: _____

Address:_____

City_____ State_____ Zip_____

Telephone _____

email address:_____

       Copies_____ @ $13.95 each =_____

Sales tax: Please add 8.25% for products
        shipped to California addresses _____

Shipping & handling $5 first book
        $3 each additional book _____

                 TOTAL_____

Payment: Check or Credit Card   Visa

Card Number_____

Name on Card_____Exp.date___/___

_____Check if you want Venna as a speaker.
_____Check to be added to an email list.